AF449348

Entrepreneurial Management

Entrepreneurial Management

GOING ALL OUT FOR RESULTS

Charles A. Dailey, Ph. D.
Dartmouth College, Hanover, New Hampshire

McGRAW-HILL BOOK COMPANY

New York   St. Louis   San Francisco   Düsseldorf
Johannesburg   Kuala Lumpur   London   Mexico
Montreal   New Delhi   Panama   Rio de Janeiro
Singapore   Sydney   Toronto

ENTREPRENEURIAL MANAGEMENT

This book was set in Baskerville linofilm by the
Vail-Ballou Press, Inc., and printed and bound by
the Vail-Ballou Press, Inc. The editors were Dale
L. Dutton, W. Hodson Mogan, and Carolyn Nagy.
The designer was Naomi Auerbach. Teresa F.
Leaden supervised production.

To John Reneau Dow

Contents

Preface

This is a book about managerial courage. Most books for managers seem to be technical and not about the guts required for risk taking. The most essential type of management is the entrepreneurial. But it is the kind we hear about the least. So it is necessary to say more about the manager as a man of nerve. There are two ways to write about managerial courage. There are inspirational books which give a brief lift. The other way—which I prefer—is to write about managerial courage. This means to get a clear picture of how managers live and work in the entrepreneurial style.

Such managers often have an uphill battle. If they are lucky enough to have a boss who values enterprise, the boss himself may be fighting an uphill battle against a board which does not. Or worse, that boss or board may have inherited an organization form which discourages enterprise. By this I mean the organization form some call bureaucracy.

The first chapter compares the entrepreneurial way of looking at organizations in the bureaucratic way. This contrast is made throughout the book, but not in order to advocate "more entrepreneurs" and "fewer bureaucrats." It is not quite that simple—every big organization requires a certain critical mass of bureaucrats for survival. Rather, the problem is to work with the bureaucrat without giving up the essential power of enterprise.

Chapter 2 goes on to describe the stresses and strains placed on entrepreneurs by the rapid rate of change in economy and society. Chapter 3 focusses on a special stress—that of conflict. The management of conflict in big corporations, a talent which the new entrepreneur should cultivate, is the theme of Chapter 4. Chapter 5 takes a new look at stress and finds that its negative effects have been exaggerated, and that the manager can transform stress into something positive.

As many firms have become set in their bureaucratic ways, Chapter 6 tells what a chief executive can do to rebuild an organization so that it reacts well to the positive stresses of risk.

The entrepreneurial style of managing has consequences for certain staff functions. Beginning with the training function in Chapter 7, these consequences are reviewed, not only with regard to training managers to be entrepreneurs but also with lowering the bureaucratic emphasis of some training departments. Chapter 8 looks at selection in a two-level manner: finding the right person to put in entrepreneurial posts and doing that selecting in an entrepreneurial manner. The last in this trio of chapters, Chapter 9, tackles the key question among all key questions: What can actually be done to improve the performance of a manager?

We are well into the last third of the twentieth century

and it is interesting to compare the entrepreneurial man at the close of the last century with the kind of man we need for this one. Enterprise still seems to be a game of economics, power, stress, and brains as before, but all these characteristics of the managerial style are being rapidly redefined under new conditions. Both individuals and corporations, according to Chapter 10, must recognize, develop, empower, and reward a new type of entrepreneur or else the economic and perhaps political world will fall into the hands of bureaucrats.

Charles A. Dailey

Acknowledgments

Many, many thanks to the managers and friends whose wisdom and counsel were so freely given me. To Marvin Bower and Paul Herzog for the opportunity to get to know European managers. To Lou Mobley for the brilliance of his exposition of management theory, and to Bob Ohmann, as sage a thinker who ever translated behavioral sciences into managerial wisdom. To Gordon Roberts, whose wit and talents in law, engineering, and so many other fields made me see new interconnections. To Quinter Miller, for chances to learn new fields of management. To Nat Baily, for his zeal for the teaching of managers. To Fred Dyer, who started teaching me to write, and Carolyn Mullins, who continued the job. And the production of this manuscript was one of creative collaboration between my wife, Ann, and Donna Musgrove.

chapter one

Competing Styles of Management

INTRODUCTION

Every manager needs his own managerial style. If he develops one which fits his personality and is realistic, it will release his energies. If he chooses one which does not, he will feel "boxed in" and be ineffective. A manager can choose an appropriate style if he understands the nature of the entrepreneurial impulse, which is the motivation that relates managers to the outer world, or environment. This need to understand the entrepreneurial impulse is one principal theme of this book.

The second is the organization's relation to the entrepreneurial impulse. Organizations cannot generate entrepreneurial impulses, but they *can* stifle them, and if they stifle these impulses, organizations become nothing more than reactive machines. Such machines survive only on the whims of the economic and political environment.

This book considers both the individual manager and the manager as part of the organization; they cannot be understood separately.

Management Theory and Risk Taking

J. Servan-Schreiber,[1] French Deputy and advocate of European unity, in *The American Challenge,* confronts Europeans with the possibility that their economic system is deteriorating under the invasion of American business. This new Normandy invasion cannot be held back, he says, because it is not an aggression. It is a *challenge* which can be countered only by a creative response. He then outlines a response in terms of political and economic reform, social justice, and increased investment in human resources.

When I had the opportunity to discuss his ideas with a diverse group of European managers, a rather different focus emerged from the discussion than Servan-Schreiber's book suggested to many readers. Our focus came to rest on risk taking as the heart of the European problem, one example being the difficulty of raising capital for new enterprises in some parts of Europe. It is not true that American institutions honor and reward risk taking, while European institutions do not. Rather, both economies should recognize that (1) risk taking is a central problem for both, and (2) we should learn together how to foster it while simultaneously protecting society and particular firms from the various excesses of the entrepreneurial impulse.

In brief, the central problem for management theory (not only in business but in the public sector as well) is risk taking. No person seriously interested in management theory can afford to limit himself to the economic aspect of risk taking nor can he leave it out. Risk is both a state of the manager's mind —a matter of courage and calculation—and a fact about the outer world. It is thus psychological as well as economic. It is also sociological in that the study of organizations (managers do not exist without organizations) is a sociological problem. Risk taking is, finally, not indifferent to statistics, in the sense that the future is always a matter of probability; but we will also be concerned with the emotions of managers, without which they would be nothing but low-speed computers.

Organization Theory and Entrepreneurs

An organization's structure is the house it builds around the entrepreneurial, or risk-taking, impulse. The walls in it, figuratively speaking, were put there to prevent some earlier miscalculation from being made again. The managers' experience became crystallized in the form of the houses in which they work. These are, for some managers, houses built in fear of making the same costly mistake twice, and I will deal frankly with the effect of fear in stifling entrepreneurial impulses (particularly as it holds back the young manager).

In short, managers and organizations are interrelated not only intellectually but irrationally. An organization cannot be understood without reference to human emotion, a fact which is ignored by most of the rather bland theories of organization now in print.

Various structures—chains of command, rules of communication, pay systems—come into being because somebody originally wanted to make some new product or expand a service, courses of action which usually involve taking some risk. The organization does *not* take risks, however; *people* do. We must examine the risk bearer in order to arrive at a picture of why the organization is the way it is. The risk taker bears the same relation to his organization that a river's source bears to its delta. One could study the delta alone, but this would not enable him to forecast the river's flood stages and droughts.

In brief, then, I am especially concerned with organization

theory's neglect of the entrepreneur and will focus attention on this particular kind of manager.

Managers Who Are Not Risk Takers

Some managers are not risk takers. A risk taker is a manager whose courses of action *might* have profitable or favorable consequences in the outer world. Some managers are technicians whose work products primarily serve other managers and workers; they cannot be entrepreneurs because they do not have "feedback" from the outside world or "market."

Other managers could be risk takers but have cultivated a bureaucratic frame of mind. These managers constitute a serious problem for corporations and public enterprises both in the United States and in Western Europe when they become either too numerous or too dominant. There is a "critical mass" below which too few bureaucrats exist and above which are too many (or too many in key places). There are ways to identify that critical point for particular organizations. That point may differ subtly from one organization to another (e.g., a public utility's would probably differ from an airframe manufacturer's). And it may even change from one point in time to the next; for example, as urbanization and social complexity increase, organizations which could formerly tolerate a great amount of risk-avoidant management will suffer from it. Consider the American electric-power industry which has suddenly become subjected to great pressure for change and very great risk.

The technical manager who avoids risks is a special problem. We will consider him when we examine some aspects of R&D administration.

CONCEPTS OF MANAGEMENT

Historically, several conflicting ways of talking about the problems of management have developed. One school emphasizes the rational problems, the *things* which are managed. Production units, sales, inventories, dollars can be counted and calculations can be made. If one thinks of them as the whole of management, he conceives of the organization as a machine—a set of interacting parts. However, there are two schools of thought about the machine: the one uses the traditional *principles of management,* as they have come to be articulated within areas of things, such as marketing, production, and finance; the other school finds these traditional areas too demarcated and the rules of thumb too crude for the giant complex corporation and draws upon the *management sciences* for advanced tools of analysis.

No manager can avoid the irrational side of management, the strong emotions, feelings, and conflicts people have. If only for the reason that people do not always do what the principles of management say they ought to do, managers have to consider the people who are managed or coordinated. If one thinks of the organization as a set of interacting people, is this image (from a logical standpoint) too different from the image of a set of interacting production, sales, or financial units? Cannot one calculate the relations among persons as well as the relations among things?

The answer is: Not always easily, and at any rate not with the same conceptual tools. One turns to the principles, concepts, and methods of *group dynamics* if he wishes to understand the relationships among persons of whom he has some direct knowledge—the group he supervises or among whom his own work is coordinated. However, such groups are confined in size and space to about the size of a jury at most; what about the analysis of the feelings, attitudes, and behavior of the far larger complexes of people who do not interact directly? Is it possible to analyze attitudes, feelings, and behavior in the giant corporate complex itself? For this analysis, he turns to the principles, concepts, and methods of *social systems.*

We therefore arrange the major methods for the analysis of management under these headings:

1. Calculation of relations among things
    a. principles of management
    b. management sciences
2. Calculation of relations among persons
    a. group dynamics
    b. social systems

This arrangement suggests two variables that are implicit in what has just been said. First, there is the question whether the organization may be treated as a machine and/or should be considered human.

The other variable is found within (1) and (2): it seems to be complexity. The principles of management are said to be simple and straightforward—forged intuitively through generations of experience in operating organizations. This does not mean that they are not useful or that they contain no information. On the other hand, the argument for the management sciences (for systems analysis, for example) is that some problems of calculating the relations among things are too subtle and have too many pitfalls for such traditional analysis.

The same variable of complexity is found within the calculations of relations among persons. Groups such as are analyzed by the principles of group dynamics are normally no larger than jury size. One turns to social systems analysis for the study of relations between divisions, departments, plants, competing companies, and so on.

Briefly, the variables may be represented in terms of two assumptions:

1. That the organization is a rational machine, or that it is a relatively nonrational entity.
2. That it is small (simple), or large and complex.

Now, following the reasoning of Koontz [2] in his classic paper, we can see where the confusion or "management theory jungle" can arise. It arises whenever a manager or behavioral scientist tries to use all these concepts at once. The four groups of concepts make different assumptions (Figure 1.1); to mix them up will lead to a certain amount of intellectual indigestion.

The indigestion is made much worse if one tries to decide which one set of concepts is "right." The proper question is rather: What is the situation, and in such a situation, which set of concepts will be most useful?

Now, I hope to show that we cannot do without all four sets of concepts. The behaviorist who attempts to study business or public administration without the aid of the traditional principles of organization is doing an understandable thing, but it is quite impossible. The converse is true: the treatment of organizations as machines is a dangerous illusion.

Part of the time, the managers of every organization have very strong feelings about what they are doing, and those feelings influence their decisions. There are fights and conflicts; the executive suite has to have soundproof walls to disguise the shouting that sometimes goes on. One writer described the

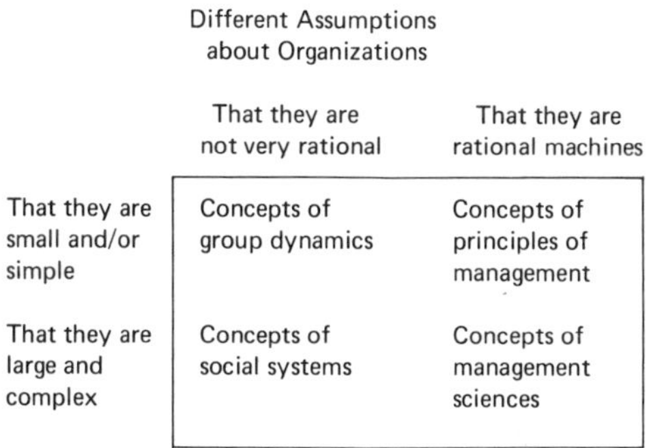

Figure 1.1

typical executive conference in his corporation as a "dog fight under a blanket." Such men have strong drives. It is foolish to pretend that they are not emotional about some of the things they do.

The Rational Machine. At other times the organization seems to be made up of managers and employees who do what they are supposed to do. When they do this, certain results can be calculated: sales, production levels, delivery schedules, costs, purchases, inventories, the *things* of life of the organization. If one cannot calculate these things, he cannot make any economic forecasts at all. One may complain about such "mechanistic thinking" all he wishes, but no firm can stay alive (or agency stay within its budget and its charter) without the ability to calculate these things.

The rational language one uses to talk about the things of management is different from the language one uses to talk about the people. The rational language is concerned with the hard data and decisions of managers; the nonrational language, with the soft data, or the emotions and motivations involved in the decisions which they make.

Why Not Just the "Machine"?

It seems more practical to calculate the relations among hard facts about the things of management than to understand the soft data about the relationships of people. Since human relationships are not calculable, being nonrational, the argument goes, let's build stronger management sciences, and the human relations can take care of themselves.

In the first place, it is not true that human relations are not calculable. An elementary acquaintance with psychology or sociology, or even a review of one's own experience, will reveal many relationships which are predictable. The predictions are not exact, but they are exact enough for decision making.

In the second place, the argument for management interest in human relationships rests precisely on the point that people did *not* do what they were expected. For the things of management to fail, people very often have to fail to do the expected. Plans were not completed; budgets were ignored; costs rise—behind many (sometimes most) of these deviations from what had been expected and calculated is the brute, unavoidable fact that somebody did not do what the plans called for or assumed; somebody ignored the budget; somebody exceeded his cost.

The "Is" and the "Ought"

The behavioral sciences (including group dynamics and social systems, but there are of course others) describe the way people are, and what they do, whether we like it or not. They are concerned with the "Is" of organizational analysis.

The rational sciences (including principles of management and management sciences) describe how we would like the things of management (the business functions, products, money) to behave, and indeed how they must behave if we are to stay alive economically. The rational sciences of management are concerned with the "Ought" of organizational analysis.

The Oughts of management are budgets, plans, policies, procedures, and principles. The facts of life are that *people* fail to meet budgets, deviate from plans, ignore policies, forget procedures, and violate principles.

The point is that this tension between the Is and the Ought is not just a manager's chief problem; it is the only reason he probably exists at all. There would be no real reason for a manager if precise plans and policies were ever certain; owners would invest and reap automatic returns if the investments were economically wise; governments could pass laws and would not require much in the way of an executive branch.

Later in this book, we will discuss quite frankly the problem of emotional stress in managerial work. Stress is inevitable because of the conflict between the Is and the Ought. There is always a variance, always a gap. The unstressed manager is not a manager at all, only a utopian fiction.

Some Managers Question the Study of Behavior

In the light of the above, it seems incredible that some managers wonder why someone thinks they should study behavior as well as business principles and technology. These managers are well aware that there is a set of concepts to be learned with regard to accounting, finance, marketing, and production (the rational machine).

In my discussions with European managers, I found some especially inclined to concentrate on the managerial languages in the rational column. They did not resist the new idea of behavioral languages (at the level of both groups and social systems), but they did, reasonably enough, request some convincing argument as to what the study of behavior would give them that they could not do without.

The only answer again is: Without "nonrational" organizational behavior, no management would exist because there is no managerial problem without this gap between the Is and the Ought.

The study of behavioral realities is vital for managers who do not wish bitter surprises and disappointments. Almost every corporation I have ever known was surprised at least once by a strike which, in hindsight, they could see coming.

The Pretensions of Behavioral Theory

It would be equal folly for a manager to study group dynamics and social systems and neglect the study of production and other such processes. Production plans, policies, schedules tell us how people ought to behave if they are going to produce within certain specifications.

If the belief that organizations are rational machines is

naïve, the theory that psychological and sociological accounts can explain organizations is foolish.

There is no competition among these languages in reality; it is only among specialized academicians that the competition could be taken seriously.

Bureaucratic versus Entrepreneurial Styles

Now let us consider an ideal type of manager who may be rare, but who must be developed, in a corporation which hopes to be long-lived. We want to know how the entrepreneur thinks, feels, and acts, indeed, how he must think, feel, and act, given an uncertain environment.

The logic of entrepreneurial thought, if not its less-rational aspect, is well described by Peter Drucker.[3] A style of life is demanded by an entrepreneurial career which is not understood by some and is frightening to many.

We will not attempt to judge the entrepreneur. I will not say he is good, happy, deserving, or brilliant, but only that he is essential and that some authorities wonder if his style is not the chief distinction between European and American management.

He is essential because he links the corporation with its environment, the public agency with its constituency, and this is the clue to understanding how he operates. He is, therefore, the link between organizational theory and the theory of the business (or other) environment.

The Language of Entrepreneurs

The entrepreneur speaks a language which enables him to compare the Ought and the Is, because his role is to bring the desirable future into being. This in turn requires him to speak a language which refers to the environment as well as the organization because only environmental response can tell him what is desirable in his products or services. In politics, the "environmental response" is votes; in business, sales; in medicine, cures. All these—votes, sales, and cures—are responses outside the direct mechanical cause-and-effect control of the politician, businessman, and physician. Since environmental response is inherently less controllable, it is less predictable. Hence, the essential element in the entrepreneur, the kind of manager who creates a desirable future, is risk. Nonentrepreneurial managers also compare the Ought and the Is, but not all of them are concerned with this kind of risk, and it is possible to play the game of management at a very low level of risk of failure. One way to do this is to measure one's results, not against an uncertain future and an uncontrollable environment, but against policies and procedures. This is the bureaucratic style of management, which is not a European monopoly; we know much about bureaucrats in the United States; both corporations and government have them. There are probably no firms that lack bureaucrats, for the simple reason that they play an essential function.

Two Definitions of Organization

Perhaps the entrepreneur can best be described by contrast with the bureaucrat. In general, the entrepreneur sees his organization as an instrument of purpose for changing something in the environment: creating a new market, improving an old one, solving a social problem, providing a new service, etc. The entrepreneurial view of an organization, for reasons that will become clear, sees it as a living being, growing because it is change-seeking, and infused with personality. The bureaucrat sees his organization as an impersonal machine or legal entity governed by rules and policies, not by people.

Entrepreneurs see organizations as living because they often create them; they develop an affection for them but are not always surprised when the time comes for one to die, combine with a second, or change its fundamental character.

Bureaucrats see organizations as eternal because they inherit them. They see organizations as stable because this is the way their ideal world is. They are rudely shocked by excessive change and deviation and long to set things "right"; failing in this, they deem it prudent to change policy so that the lawful character, their "reality," will be preserved.

Origins of the Two Styles

The entrepreneurial style grows out of the search for opportunity in the environment. Such a manager says, "Ah, there's something out there that could be done." He is an environmentally oriented innovator. Every new firm or agency is initially entrepreneurial; then, as has often been pointed out, if it survives, the second-generation heads may change its style quite a bit.

The first-generation chief executive may have made some serious mistakes or be in serious difficulty, as was Durant about 1920 in General Motors.[4] He is then succeeded, often, by a second-generation, more professional manager. This man often may find it difficult to avoid overreacting to the excesses or omissions of his predecessor. There is a temptation to substitute an impersonal, bureaucratic style of management for the personal, possibly autocratic, dynamic style of the first chief. Accounts suggest that this happened to General Dynamics Corporation in the transition from its first architect to his successor.[5]

The trends to bureaucratic management can also be illustrated in the history of the United States Civil Service. In the nineteenth century, the autocratic practices of elected politicians were to use federal jobs as "spoils," or rewards, for their supporters. The Congress began to exempt federal jobs from this system by placing them under tight regulation by the Civil Service Commission, but still more, it reacted to the autocratic excesses of the spoils system by creating one of the world's larger bureaucracies.

Thus bureaucratic managers and practices sweep into power in reaction to the excesses of autocrats, just as laws are written in response to violence. One effect of this process is to encourage a conception within the organization that it must prevent excess, maintain control, and preserve resources. This conception can result in a defensive organization.

The bureaucratic style, then, grows out of the experience that one can control excess with rules and prevent irrationality by policy. An example comes to mind. A plant manager fired an older employee whom he considered incompetent on the Friday just preceding the Monday on which the employee's pension became vested. There was a hue and cry from the higher management (as well as in the plant) which reversed the decision. The damage done, both to the plant's human relations and to the manager's authority, was so severe that the corporation considered whether it should pass a rule to prevent this from "ever happening again."

But consider what such a rule would be. Would the rule say, "An employee may not be fired within six months of the date of pension vesting"? This merely vests the pension at an earlier date. Does the rule say that employees over sixty may not barely miss having their pensions vested? This has the effect of vesting a pension earlier if one is sixty, and leaves us uncertain as to the protection if one is fifty-nine.

Almost any rule would complicate the pension vesting without necessarily avoiding new moral outrages. But the bureaucratic preference, nevertheless, is to pass the rule and to let additional rules take care of the new problems and hazards.

In brief, then: entrepreneurial styles develop from opportunistic perceptions of the environment. Bureaucratic styles develop from moral outrage and error.

Measurement Used by Each Style

Because the entrepreneur and the bureaucrat are trying to do different things, they use different criteria for judging performance. Indeed, they do not even judge the same performance.

Because the bureaucrat is seeking to prevent deviations within the organization, he studies internal phenomena primarily: records what people are doing and where they put their time; seeks to find out whether they are following policy and procedure, spending within limits, doing what is the job description. He values such measurements as almost an end in themselves. As the qualities of *impersonal* and *objective* are present throughout his style of management, these qualities are also found within his measuring system. He is quite fond of personnel testing for this reason.

Because the entrepreneur is seeking results in the outer world, he looks at external phenomena and at what the outside world does in response to his products or services. In attempting to learn what that world thinks, feels, and does about his products or services, he is often content with an intuitive impression if he cannot obtain objective facts. This is not to say that he is not tough-minded, but rather that, as a specialist in the future, he must necessarily be more content at times with intangible indices. He sometimes lives on hope, which is too thin a diet for the bureaucrat.

The bureaucrat reserves his soft-mindedness for ultimate questions. He is willing to assume that an irrelevant but precise measure is better than a relevant but vague one. A classic example is in Blau's study of a large federal agency which decided to measure the effectiveness of interviewers by counting the number of interviews each completed per day regardless of the effectiveness of the interviews in getting jobs for the clients.[6,7] My colleagues and I happened to study that same agency and encountered a similar example. The agency had invested, and spent, $6 million on a training program before someone demanded that it be evaluated by an external result.[8] The advocates of training evaluation in Congress reported a prevailing disinterest on the part of agencies in evaluating such results; [9] a similar charge was directed toward industrial training, although a recent book indicates a change of attitude.[10]

Equally frightening examples may be produced in American universities. For example, we now know that medical school grades are unrelated to later performance of a medical student as a physician.[11] College grading, generally, seems to serve purposes of internal bureaucratic control rather than evaluation against external and subsequent effects.

There are, in fact, few instances in which a college grade is related to any kind of human performance except other college grades.[12]

These internal preoccupations are reflected in cost systems. The cost systems of bureaucrats are directed toward measuring the consumption of resources. Costs can be evaluated by the entrepreneur only in an investment context—in proportion to ultimate payoff.

The bureaucratic and entrepreneurial systems differ in regard to what performance they measure, how precisely they measure it, and why they measure performance.

Structural Principles

The bureaucratic organization is based on ideas of structure obtained from the military, which perhaps got them from earlier feudal structure. In such a structure, there is a single unified chain of command, and the oversimplified notion that, in Boulding's verse,

> In every modern corporation
> are channels of communication
> along which lines, from foot to crown,
> reports flow up and vetoes down.

Functions are shown in boxes, and fairly stable lines of authority are drawn from the "crown" down to the "dukes," then to "barons," and eventually to first-line "counts."

In contrast, the entrepreneurial manager, who may neglect to read the organization chart given him by the personnel department, has a rather different image of the organization. It is based more upon his greater interest in commerce with the environment (in which case he is more interested in drawing pictures of trading transactions or trading areas) or in producing some kind of new product or service (in which case his organizational doodling will resemble a PERT chart more than it will, say, hierarchy). He is more likely to be preoccupied with images of action than of power, and his diagrams will show teams or clusters of people working temporarily on projects, as in R&D project management. The entrepreneurial manager may be influenced by military imagery, also, but if so, it is more the image of guerrilla tactics and strategy than of close-order drill.

In brief, the entrepreneurial image of an organization is more likely to be a marketing or an R&D model than a production diagram. The image of production precision and control probably guides the bureaucrat's thinking about organizations, especially mass production.

The task of the entrepreneurial organization structure is to obtain some kind of favorable response (e.g., a sale), while the bureaucratic structure is concerned with production and getting things done within set limits.

Management by "Exception" *versus* "Objective"

Some American corporations have attempted to install a system in which managers set objectives and measure results against them. Managers and all employees are then judged against those objectives, in the sense intended by Peter Drucker.[13] In spite of the obvious rationality of this approach, the resistance to it can border upon the phenomenal.

An example was the initiative of Robert McNamara, who introduced "cost effectiveness" to the United States government through the Defense Department. The effectiveness of an operation, procedure, or system was to be determined against its external results. A reasonable cost was one which seemed in proportion to those results. The concept is similar to that of return on investment but is generalized to public agencies.

The cost-effectiveness system met a wall of incomprehension for much the same reason that management-by-objectives programs sometimes encounter resistance (if less obvious) in corporations:

1. Management by objectives is a risk-taking approach and is therefore naturally resisted by those accustomed to operate at lower risks.

2. Many managers have been nurtured in the bureaucratic tradition and can sincerely say that they find such a system incomprehensible.

The bureaucratic manager operates by exception rather than by objectives of obtaining environmental response or of achieving opportunities in the day-to-day world outside the organization. (This is not to say that everyone who manages by exception is a bureaucrat; it *is* to say that it is the only management style open to the bureaucrat.)

Try to understand his attitude: the system of the bureaucrat is to seek to control the operations under his direct surveillance, and this is usually feasible. He can control his expenses. He can apply a well-written law. He can follow a well-designed procedure. He can assure that his people work from nine to five. To propose that he drop this precise system for a less certain one in which he must go to "the field" or the outer environment in order to measure his performance is an appalling idea. He would be rash to agree to substitute an imprecise, risky (though relevant) set of measurements for a precise, less risky (if not always relevant) set of internal measures.

The entrepreneur labors under the immense disadvantage

of seeking responses from an environment which is outside his control because it is biologically, socially, physically, and legally separate from himself. Such management by environmental objectives is a high-risk style of management.

Time Perspectives

The bureaucratic view of the future hopes that it will continue the past (project last year's costs for next year's budgets, plus an allowance for error and cost increases). Good management means a constant future which one seeks to achieve through wise design of rules and precise control systems. The past is limit for the future. Precedent, custom, agreed-on policies—these are the aids to memory of the bureaucrat and help him document his analysis of the present performance.

To the entrepreneur, the future is occasion for something different, a time for realization of the opportunities presently perceived in the environment. He is naturally disposed to change and expects it. The violent ups and downs of profit and fortune may depress and elate him as much as they do the bureaucrat, but they do not surprise or frighten him. To the entrepreneur, the past is a good example of what can happen, rather than a boundary for what will happen. It is a foundation, a "takeoff platform," for change rather than a source of future stability.

At this point, no doubt, the impression of the bureaucrat is a negative one. This is not the intention. There are values in bureaucracy. We cannot forget, for example, the humanity which there is in the very procedures for avoiding excess by willful, ignorant, or autocratic entrepreneurs.

Attitudes toward Change

In consequence of their definition of time, these two styles of management view change in two different ways. The important thing for bureaucrats is to develop a stable structure, to

minimize precipitous and costly change. The important thing
for the entrepreneur is to choose his change and seek it. He is
a change maker, a mover, and shaker.

The bureaucrat, as a result, is the great balance wheel of the
corporation. The entrepreneur is restless, keeps others emotionally "up" by constantly innovating; however, the entrepreneur differs from a merely restless and discontented manager
because his restlessness is reserved for environmental targets.

Overall Views of Organization and Environment

The bureaucratic view can be briefly characterized as more
concerned with the organization than with the environment,
and the entrepreneurial view, the opposite.

It is commonly supposed that the top executive provides the
entrepreneurial view, and the middle management the bureaucracy. In the United States government, for example, the policy heads of major agencies change with the party in power;
reporting to them are the federal bureaucratic executives.

It is misleading to think of entrepreneurs as only "top-
drawer" men. It is a style which, in theory, can be found at
any level in contact with the external world. There may be organizations in which the entrepreneurs are on the firing line,
with the top executives insulated from the environment.

The entrepreneurial style, in brief, can be used by anyone,
since it is an attitude toward work itself. To convey the flavor
of that attitude, I sometimes use the word "teleological," from
the Greek *telos,* for purposive. General comparisons between
the bureaucratic and the purposive or teleological styles of
work and organization are summarized in Figure 1.2.*

---

* Figure 1.2 owes much to many discussions I have had with Louis
Mobley of IBM. He has given a stimulating lecture on the contrasting
"world views" of these two styles of management, which unfortunately has
never been published.

Bureaucratic versus Entrepreneurial Styles
of Management

	Bureaucratic style	Entrepreneurial (or teleocratic) style
Definition	Organization viewed as an impersonal machine governed by rules, not people.	Organization viewed as a living being, growing and change-seeking, infused with personality.
Origins	Excesses of industrial revolution and of spoils system in politics.	An innovative idea for a product, service, or realization of an opportunity.
Purposes of organization	Control behavior and prevent excess.	Release human energies by presenting opportunities which call them forth.
Measurement	Measure internal occurrences, especially deviations from plan, policy, or budget.	Evaluate environmental responses to the organization's actions or products.
Structural principles	Hierarchic, derived from military and/or from mass-production models.	Process, project, and goal-oriented, derived from marketing or R&D models.
Objectives of work	The work itself.	The effects of the work.
View of the future	The future is a continuation of the past; desirable future is a continuation of the past.	The future is what is possible, in realizing its opportunities.
The past	Limits the future.	Example of what can happen but not seen as a limit.
Attitude toward change	Stability is more important than change.	The most important thing is to choose which changes will be most productive and to seek them.

Figure 1.2

OTHER STYLES

There are other managerial styles. The teleocrat (the entrepreneur at any level, not just the boss) is not an autocrat, because the autocrat or managerial dictator is disinterested in a report of the results of his policies. He commands the world, while the teleocrat is a sensitive observer.

The teleocrat has particular difficulties with participative management. If he needs to consult with either subordinates or associates who are basically oriented to stable, mechanistic, or self-perpetuating values, he faces serious compromises of his style. This need not happen but often does. However, a work force which was responsive to the market would make better entrepreneurial decisions than a bureaucratic owner. This is the issue rather than that of industrial democracy versus the rights of capital.

The teleocrat has an uneasy alliance with the technocratic style. For example, a creative engineer whose impulse is to innovate may have such a strong urge to innovate that he goes beyond the bounds of any relation to organizational purposes. However, the best technical and scientific minds are innovative, and they undoubtedly can communicate more readily with the teleocrat than with the bureaucrat.

The Teleological Generalist

As generalists, the entrepreneurs and teleocrats of an organization do not fit neatly into any of the language boxes drawn earlier (Figure 1.1). They quite obviously do not think of their organizations as impersonal machines; that is the bureaucratic "bag." But quite clearly, generalists cannot be psychologists and sociologists; the latter are technocrats.

Generalists can be shown as a third dimension in this diagram. While difficult to show on a printed page, we may perhaps suggest their nature with the following diagram, which says that the entrepreneur must speak some part of each of the four languages shown:

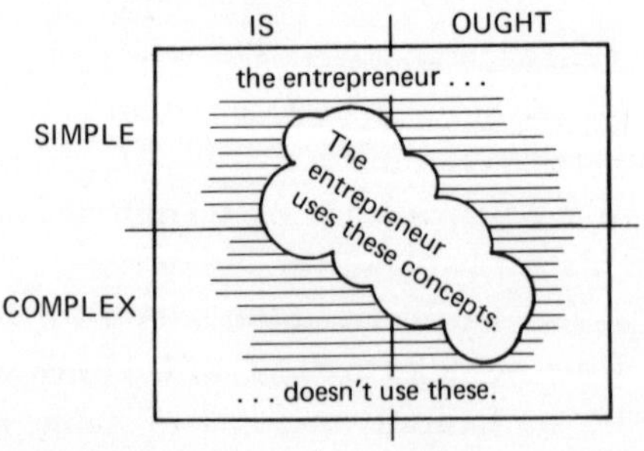

The new entrepreneur (that is, the manager capable of building large-scale, innovative organizations in the urban, technical, world-village, rapidly changing, and occasionally violent society which seems ahead of us in the next three decades) is different from the old entrepreneur. The word "teleocratic" might serve to mark this change. He is different in that he must speak all these languages, not only the language of profit-loss and nineteenth-century capitalism.

He must be somewhat more educated, then, than the old entrepreneur, but perhaps not so well educated as the specialists in management. Surely he can be more responsible than the old entrepreneurs if he is more sophisticated in his grasp of the environment as a system in which the political, social, and other side effects (or "fallout") from economic change must be much better calculated than in the past. He will be economist, behavioral scientist, businessman, and systems man, all rolled into one. I can't say that I have met any such manager as yet, but I am certain that he is essential to the process of running cities and building world firms. Since such managers are essential, we must hope they exist.

chapter two

Managing Change

Managers take risks because they want to realize opportunities. Every time a manager does so, he creates a new set of problems for himself and his organization. This chapter assumes that these manager-created problems are better for the organization than other kinds of problems. For example, the bureaucratic manager also faces problems, but they are not of his own making. They result from policy failures, increasing costs, technical problems, and so on. It is the nature of bureaucracy to be reactive, to wait for problems.

The issue is: Whose headache do you prefer? The answer of the entrepreneur is that in general it is better to have his own headache. The risk taker not only chooses his own headaches —those resulting from deliberate opportunity seeking—but also the timing at which they will occur. Self-controlled pain

in general hurts less than pain which others give. The dentist
operates on this principle when he gives the patient a way to
signal that he stop drilling.

Investment theory does not distinguish between those investment plans which are opportunity-seeking and those plans
which are reactive, or problem-solving. We can't prove it, but
strongly suspect—on psychological grounds—that the first
kind of plans provides better returns. If so, the reason is the
different style of management involved. Let's explore that
style.

MANAGING THE FUTURE

Books for or about managers very often save the "future" for
the last chapter. Today's future, however, is already upon us.
Society is changing so rapidly that earlier habits of thought—
which held that something called "long-range planning" could
be done in relaxed, creative fashion because the planner had a
five to ten years' period in which to make up his mind—are
being replaced by a new discipline called "futurology." This
chapter is not for futurologists but does attempt to define the
kind of management which is future-oriented. That manager
is the kind who knows there are all around him, *now* existing,
visible trends whose full effects will not appear for one or two
decades. In this sense, the future is here. There are many sages
to tell you how different it will be in 2000—some say the
world of 2000 will differ from 1970 as much as the world of
1500 differed from 1970. The details boggle the mind. For example, consider the forecast of average family income of $15,-
000 (in present dollars, too); we hardly know how to react to
it. But these mind-bogglers are not our main concern. Instead,
consider the visible present trends, such as air pollution, population growth, urban concentration. What kind of management analyzes these present and all-too-visible trends to find
opportunities in them?

First of all, this kind of future manager must be a man for "now." He lives in the present. He is not waiting for the marvels of the year 2000. But it is a different kind of "now" from the "now" of the bureaucrat. He sees, in the present, things happening which are new, different, and will be even more so in the future. The bureaucrat looks for sameness, and his managerial techniques are oriented to the exception—to finding and eliminating deviations. The entrepreneur looks out the window and sees timber *now* growing in a forest which will be harvested in a generation; the bureaucrat not only misses the forest but can't imagine the harvest.

It is false to say that the entrepreneur is a dreamer and that the bureaucrat is practical and operational. Rather, the risk taker is trying to be practical over a different time period than the bureaucrat.

The entrepreneur not only sees the clues for the future but responds to them faster. If he waits until a trend is an obvious and overwhelming opportunity, everyone else also sees it. By then there is not only more competition, but the level of competition will be harassed, cheap, and frantic, a game not usually worth playing. This fast, early response is made at a point when clues to the future are subtle. They are inherently more risky for this reason. What kind of man takes these risks?

Life Style *versus* Managerial Style

"Life style" is a term usually applied to hippies. But we all have a life style. The life style of most of us is called "square" by the hippies and the young. However, the term life style was invented by Alfred Adler, the psychoanalyst. It refers not to the length of his beard but to a person's whole way of life: what he is trying to do.

The average reader of a book on management may expect simple rules and maxims for doing business. Why talk about deeper questions such as life style? The principal reason is in the very nature of being an entrepreneur. Being a risk-taking manager is a broader commitment to make. The bureaucrat, like the average white-collar employee is said to be, is oriented to carrying out specific actions within a specific set of guidelines, for a price, from nine to five. It is not so difficult to develop rules, principles, and even a simple technology for being a bureaucrat, or an employee. Entrepreneurs, however, have a strategy for living and working which is distinctive. It is so individualistic that it would be presumptuous for me to describe it. But there are some things which should be said about this life style. Ernest Dale [14] describes it quite well in an article of his about André Malraux. Malraux is not a manager in a literal sense, but a man who learned, in Dale's opinion, to cope with the kind of world in which we are and will be living.

Malraux and the Human Condition

Whether fighter, writer, philosopher, or Cabinet Minister of France, André Malraux has been everywhere, seen it all, in the first half of this century. If he typifies the person who is able to live effectively in a confusing, at times wildly chaotic, world of revolutionary change, his views are worth hearing. Malraux speaks about the human condition of the kind of person who wants to make a difference in this kind of world.

First, Malraux makes it plain that this kind of man is concerned with his whole life; he is asking questions about life style and not just about a set of techniques for getting little things done. He is asking some very basic questions about himself and not about being an "employee."

Second, Malraux addresses us as a man of strong feelings and definite actions. This is emphatically not the image of a manager one receives from reading most of the rational books on managers. But the rational books are misleading. The manager, riding his train from the suburbs, is more likely to be thinking about his tragedies and triumphs than he is to be thinking the bland thoughts of the man depicted in Whyte's *Organization Man*.[15] A character of Malraux's puts the issue to the rational thinkers this way:

> What good to me are all those thoughts of yours if you can't give my tragedy a thought? What you do, all of you, is much more to the point than what you say. You guys are all too intellectual.[16]

The activist manager will understand this language. Malraux's own life was activist—fighting in China, Spain, and France. And so his conclusions about the limitations upon activism—practical get-it-done philosophy—should be of value. He tells us that the lone activist is dead. The thinking activist in this century struggles in organized groups. He joins himself to a band of colleagues who together fight for some great cause. This unity releases potential in each man; it gives him energy and an outlet for his talents.

Some managers follow this strategy for finding a place for themselves in the world. They create an organization. Malraux says, "Modern organization is much more a will to organization than to power." Why do they pour their efforts into organization building? Because this gives them a fundamental answer to the only question, according to Malraux, which is worth much of a man's time these days: "How do I make the best of my life?"

The fundamental answer is that most of us can make the best of our lives through organizations, not through lonely effort. This is a world of giant organizations, in which even the 100th corporation in the United States is more powerful than the strongest kingdom of the Middle Ages. The new entrepreneur is not a Billy Sol Estes looking for a private financial killing, nor a lone inventor, but an organizer of human talent.

Ernest Dale [14] shows us that the heroes in Malraux's novels are a new type. They find or create a "virile fraternity," overcoming solitude and finding their lives in organized action in the company of others. Their action is part of a movement or a corporation, not the lone—and largely futile—risk taking of a Don Quixote.

Obsolescence of the Organization Man

The way of life described by Malraux (an entrepreneurial way of life) is not the life of the organization man described by William Whyte. Whyte's book describes one way to be, and perhaps a very safe way to be. It may also be an accurate description, for all I know, of the way most managers do behave. Just one slight difficulty with it: it is going out of style. This is a very ominous statement, and a sweeping statement. Unfortunately, I can't offer facts to prove it. But it is a deduction which one might draw from the arguments presented by Alvin Toffler.[17]

Future Shock

Alvin Toffler uses the term "future shock" to refer to "the dizzying disorientation brought on by the premature arrival of the future."

So many things are changing at once, and so fast, that the manager's first problem is to find a target in all this confusion. Malraux's problem was not so great. When he fought in China, his enemy was clear; and the German occupation provided a clear target for the French resistance.

It is no longer a simple matter to know what or who is a "target" for a business firm. Ideas and things are too transient:

■ People: in asking "Who are my customers?" one of Peter Drucker's [13] fundamental questions, the manager has more difficulty now that one out of five Americans changes his address each year.

■ Occupations: the flight engineer's occupation lasted only 15 years; space scientists, only about 13.

■ Things: product lines, too, are transient; what is the average product life in the electronics industry? It is pretty brief.

■ Knowledge: the amount of scientific data printed every day in the world would fill several sets of the encyclopedia.

Organizations have a new transience. Between 1948 and 1968 in the United States, the rate of business acquisition of manufacturing firms rose from 223 per year to 2,300 per year. The acquired assets rose from $66 million a year to over $6 billion a year. The merger trend has become a flood.[18]

Even within the organization there is a trend toward what Toffler calls "ad-hocracy." A project team is assembled to solve a specific problem (theorists in organizational behavior call this "task-force" organization). It may not even last long. Toffler cites one example of an immense combine in space science which was deliberately set up to have a five-year life; it was, in his words, "nothing less than a disposable division—the organizational equivalent of paper dresses or throwaway tissues [p. 119f]." [17]

In this kind of world, the organization man, the bureaucrat, and other nine to five people, will not be obsolete, but I predict they will be among the principal and early victims of the future shock Toffler describes. They include the engineer among the unemployed along Boston's route 128, the Ph.D. in the suddenly overmanned teaching profession, the flight engineer, the overspecialized members of any of several hundred professions and occupations.

Shock-proof Managers

What kind of man can successfully survive the kind of life in which he may have several careers during one life span, belong to several corporations, move his confused family a dozen or more times? Quite obviously, he lives hard, takes risks, fights for something, and does all this within an organization or fraternity of risk takers. Intellectually and emotionally, he is more like the beachcomber in the Camel ad than he is like the Sloan Wilson "man in the grey-flannel suit." But unlike the beachcomber, he finds a way to "do his thing" in the urban world and doesn't run away to the South Seas or the Caribbean.

The models we have for this kind of life—sports and revolution—are exciting.[19] But they illustrate the emotional side better than the intellectual. The difficulty is that the pass defender throwing the hard tackle and the campus radical know precisely who their "enemy" is, or at least believe they do. Neither has any intellectual problem at all. The entrepreneur resembles them in their go-for-broke style but differs from them sharply in that he has an intellectual problem in defining targets in an ambiguous future. Unlike the campus radical, he must find a set of goals—something to create which is worth doing—as he is in the business of making things happen rather than preventing them from happening; he is *architect* and not anarchist.

BUILDING A NEW MANAGERIAL LIFE STYLE

To live and work well in a world of such change, especially if one belongs to a sluggish organization, will require sharp adaptation and personal growth. The manager who wants to cultivate a new managerial life style can take two steps:

1. Adopt an attitude toward his work which minimizes future shock and emphasizes calculated risk taking.
2. Cultivate the skills required to manage change.

Without the attitude, the skills are useless. If one adopts the attitude and does not cultivate the skills, the attitude is dangerous and will probably succeed only in getting him fired or driving him out of business. The two steps are clearly interlocked.

The manager who has an activist stance is prepared for aggressive action toward the future. He does not wait for change to wash over him like a tidal wave. This active stance is as necessary for him as it is for the prizefighter to be poised on the balls of his feet. A passive manager is like a fighter working from his heels; he has no protective stance and is a "setup" for the next haymaker his opponent chooses to throw. Some managers are frightened by the future. As change approaches them (*any* kind of change: in marketing, production, labor relations, merger, etc.), such managers behave like a rabbit crossing a highway at night: if he suddenly sees very bright headlights bearing down on him, he will freeze in the middle of the road and wait to be hit.

The managerial readiness for action, on the other hand, can be described in terms of these basic assumptions:

1. In a world of change, the manager's chief job is to manage change.
2. If he does not manage change, it will manage *him*.
3. Change won't manage itself.

The Chief Job of the Manager Is to Manage Change. Many managers believe that they are managing money, production, products, or people, or some combination of these. This can hardly be denied. But when we look at these things in a state of change, we find a common denominator. Managing people is usually most difficult when one is trying to get them to change. The money problem seems to peak when the conditions governing its flow are changing and new initiatives are required. The problem with markets is that they shift. The problem with production is that "they" (our engineers or someone else's) keep coming up with something new. In brief, the most difficult problem for the manager is change; most of the routines will take care of themselves, or the computer will handle them, or a clerk can do it. This seems to be true enough for corporations to place a premium on those who can get changes made. The term "change agent" has been used, as in a *New York Times* ad (October 7, 1963), which attempted to recruit in this way:

> What's a change agent? A result-oriented individual able to accurately and quickly resolve complex tangible and intangible problems. Energy and ambition necessary for success.

A change agent is not, however, quite the same as a manager of change. The agent tries to facilitate change by solving the problems which inevitably follow change. The manager is the one who introduced the change in the first place.

Such a manager is a mover, shaker, initiator. He introduces change, not just for the sake of change, but in the normal course of trying to realize his opportunities. He is not likely to suffer from future shock, the haymaker which the future is constantly throwing at us. He chooses to drive the car down the road rather than be the waiting rabbit.

If He Does Not Manage Change, It Will Manage Him. We all know managers who react to crises all day long. Drucker suggests that, in certain departments, up to 90 percent of the manager's time is spent with the 10 percent of his units who give him the most trouble, and sometimes with the least profitable 10 percent.[20] The "units" can be customers, or employees, or even machines. The principle is that time is not distributed in a rational manner. Some such managers are "firehouse" managers, waiting for the alarm to ring. To be sure, some departments are necessarily built like firehouses— e.g., the labor relations department—and their managers had better be able to keep their cool. Others are organized on a firehouse basis with no real reason. They put themselves at the mercy of pressures. They are managed by events. The risk taker, in contrast, has an easier time than the firehouse manager. True, he may sometimes run scared, but he generally has an easier time because he creates the events and sets off the alarms. Firebugs have more fun.

How do people become unwilling firehouse or crisis managers? Somebody created the job in the first place in such a way that the manager in that job came to believe he was supposed to operate routines and only occasionally experience pressure, do new thinking, and perhaps stick his neck out. Such a manager, by waiting for these "new things" (or exceptions) to happen, becomes a crisis manager by default. To make a terrible pun, such "default" is "de fault" of de manager.

Change Won't Manage Itself. The third aspect of the risk-taking attitude is the deliberate choice to shape the change so that it will be constructive. If he does not do so, the change-oriented manager knows, the change has a good chance to be destructive instead. Change won't manage itself; it has taken over a hundred years for us to recognize this fact. We used to assume that change was evolution; progress was inevitable; things always worked out for the best; that society and business firms would manage themselves. Anyone who has ever lived in or been in a large city can now offer a thousand exceptions to this naïve belief in social evolution. Cities are running down; crime rates are rising out of sight; smog thickens; great lakes die; all because someone was *timid* or naïve about managing change.

People outside business firms have little understanding of the task of the executive. There used to be a union song about how nice it would be to be the foreman and "watch the work done." "Real work" is traditionally considered to be labor, physical, and routine; "management" is just letting other people turn out the work. Somewhat the same naïveté confuses the image of change. For example, management is often considered to be setting a goal and then implementing it; policies are chosen to guide the implementation. Then one's managerial task is to see that the plan and the policies are followed. Management, in brief, operates the company. This view of management is true enough, just as the laboring man's view that he puts out more sweat than the manager is true enough. What is wrong with the "operating view" is its focus. Managers do set goals; do set out to implement them. But this is not the most *difficult* thing they do, and if they are wise, is not the thing to which they put their best resources of imagination and concentration.

What is most difficult is that managers set *new* goals, create *new* ways of implementing them, or find themselves compelled to *change* the implementation before it is completed. All of this makes it sound as if entrepreneurs engage in change for its own sake (they should not). Such a policy as "change for its own sake" leads to the absurdities of excessive reorganization, waste in product life, tearing down new Manhattan hotels to put up office buildings, and premature supersonic transport planes. The entrepreneur may err in the direction of change for its own sake. In spite of this, his basic motive is opportunity-seeking, which is always change-making. But not all change making is opportunity-seeking.

Skills of the Change Manager

Understanding the Innovative Process. In military history, there is an unremitting pressure to devise new hardware. The elements in that process are grim but instructive. Abundant examples may be found in Walter Millis's *Arms and the Man.*[21] Rifling was put into muskets to change the muzzle velocity and accuracy—the change in hardware. The effects: a whole wave of other changes or side effects resulting from this one alteration in hardware. The same example may be found after the introduction of the machine gun: many side effects. The typical process might be described by this sequence of events:

1. A technical change in hardware (rifling of guns, the machine gun, tanks, airplanes, atom bomb) is introduced.

2. It then requires modification of strategy, tactics, or organization, or all three. For example: barbed wire altered military tactics in World War I.

3. The modification (especially the change in military organization) leads to uncertainty, stress, and conflict. Example: air power provoked a thirty-year fight within the United States military.

4. A period of resistance ensues. In the United States, the fight against the aircraft carrier lasted well into World War II.

5. The resistance to the modification itself imposes changes on the technology or on its organizational implementation. In World War II, radar was installed on American planes in Britain but under such conditions of secrecy that the crews were not trained to use it for an inordinate period. The resistance may also halt the change altogether.

The essential problem for a manager of change is to prevent the reaction in (5) from being destructive. His essential problem is *not* to prevent all resistance; only an autocrat would think that. Resistance is normal within limits.

Resistance Management. When one introduces a major change (production method, pricing, or other change), he should expect his organization to react in a variety of ways. These are classified below (Figure 2.1). Some members of the organization can be found at every point of the "resistance spectrum." If too many collect at the left end, especially if they have power to interfere, they will be able to prevent the change, distort it, or prevent it from being effective. If too many collect at the right end, one wonders at the critical powers of the organization and if there was sufficient debate. In general, however, those to the right of the vertical dotted line are helping and those to the left hindering the particular

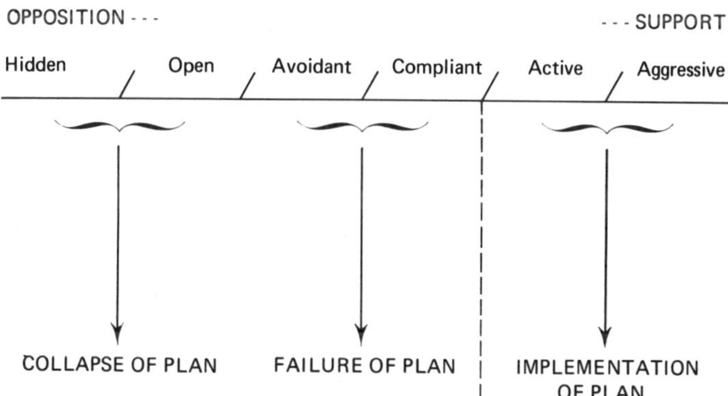

Figure 2.1

change. I would classify the "compliance" point as negative because (1) such persons are often merely waiting for the inevitable costs or unforeseen difficulties of the change to move further to the left, and (2) their brainless obedience is sometimes dangerous. In the figure, "hidden opposition" is classified as more serious than "open opposition." It poses more problems for the change manager because he cannot get data on what is happening to the change. He should be grateful if he can keep his resistance out in the open.

Resistance to change is here regarded as an inevitable side effect of change. I have never seen a major change which did not arouse resistance. It is normal for an organization. The problem is not "social engineering" to "con" the people into buying the change but rather so to manage the change that the resistance will not abort the true intent. A food-processing corporation introduced high-speed packaging machines. The new machines were installed first in a plant where the relations were good between managers and workers. This feasibility test showed better whether the equipment was sound. Had it been tested in another plant, any "failures" might really have been due to the workers' desire to see it fail or to their skepticism about the managerial intent.

PRINCIPLES FOR THE MANAGEMENT OF CHANGE

The central problem in managing change is to obtain enough resistance to ensure careful evaluation but not enough to make the net effect destructive. How is this done? Fortunately, a sufficient number of organizations have been studied to permit some rough generalizations about how change is resisted or productively implemented. Many of the following generalizations are based on the very complete summary provided by Berelson and Steiner.[22] Their book presents 1,000 generalizations about human behavior, as determined by research in economics, cultural anthropology, political science, psychology, and sociology. Many of the generalizations pertain to how behavior is changed.

Such generalizations should not be used as laws. Rather they are checkpoints for planning change. Any particular generalization will work in some cases and not in others. They are more than common sense because factually documented, but less than iron laws of behavior. Nevertheless, the reader will find many that in his own common-sense observations often do apply. He should enlarge his inventory of principles for managing change by drawing from the following list as he engages in planning where, when, how, and how fast certain changes are to be instituted. Some of the inventory suggest who should be involved in the change. Still others suggest background factors for planning it. The generalizations are:

1. *Hardware changes faster than ideas do.*

Every culture is more receptive to tangible innovation (e.g., refrigerators and automobiles) than to ideas. Ideas require more abstract intelligence and are seemingly easier to refute. This is true of Eskimos (who will buy radios but question school) and of Congress (which would rather buy a new submarine than purchase a research analysis of mental deficiency). Both would contribute, perhaps, to the national defense, but the typical Congressman would more likely understand the relevance of the sub than the research. A slum dweller is more likely to buy a TV set than to purchase a reading course; he knows he can watch the set; he is not sure about the longer-range payoff from the course.

Coca-Cola has moved around the world; democracy has not. Computers may be growing faster than new managerial information systems. If one were a corporation president and wanted to alter the decision-making systems of his executives, he could probably do it faster (even if at more expense) by buying a computer. The executives will be in awe of the computer, and while they are numbed with fascination at its immense powers, the computer programmer will slip in a new information system on them—at a hundred times greater cost, of course.

This awe at the physical and concrete is often thought to be an American trait. It is not; as best one can read the evidence of anthropologists, men everywhere are fascinated by new tools. The trait must be as old as the first flintstone.

2. *Most inventions are made by outsiders.*

This principle bears on the question, "Where should the manager look for constructive innovation?" It would be pleasant to think that the organization can and will generate its own innovations, at a sufficient rate to solve its problems and realize its opportunities. But the evidence indicates that organizations and societies do this only in a minor way. They are dependent on the creative outsider. For example, consider rural society. Most new farm implements are invented by city people! And what made American farming overwhelmingly productive was agricultural science imported via the county agent system—itself one of the most successful devices ever invented for disseminating innovation. The agricultural scientist and the farm agent in this instance are the creative outsiders. For somewhat the same reasons, corporations use outside consultants and regard a certain level of inflow of recruited employees as desirable. That is, when the "inbred" level of promotion-within is too high (over 90 percent?), the company may die. Some device has to be found for importing ideas.

3. *Innovation enters the organization fastest at the top.*

It would be pleasant to think that innovation can come into the organization at all levels. That would provide a good argument for more industrial democracy. Unfortunately, most organizations treat ideas better if they come down the hierarchy than if they go up. There is something like a principle of "social gravity": "Ideas move down the ladder of management faster than they move up."

Every worker sees things that the company ought to do differently. If a suggestion-box system is installed, and the worker-management relations are good, some of these ideas will be put forth and up the ladder. In the nature of things this system does not provide more than a minor part of the innovation needed. Consequently, every salesman wants to talk to the top man, and every salesman is right.

4. *Innovation enters through a progressive elite.*

Many different kinds of managers influence large organizations. Some are receptive to ideas, and some are not. They can be placed on a scale from a "conservative elite" at one end to a "progressive elite" at the other (Figure 2.2). The scale does not refer to their politics but rather to the character of their contact with the world outside the organization. We can make some guesses as to their makeup and background. The conservative elite are powerful men. Each of them has probably

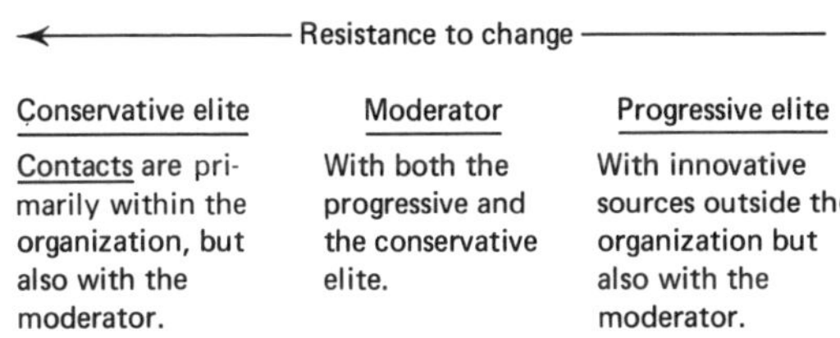

Figure 2.2

come up through the ranks and has less life outside the firm. He is a devoted student of the organization, knows it well, knows what its people can take in the way of change. He is more likely to be dedicated to maintaining organizational unity, policy compliance, and the style and traditions of the organization. The moderator is a conflict manager in communication with both extremes. The progressive elite are influential managers with rather active contacts outside the organization and even outside the industry. Such a manager is in more active contact with the world of change and of ideas, and this exposure is more likely to make him discontent with things as they are. He communicates more frequently with inventors and idea men, and even will have lunch with advertising agency people. The problem of innovation posed by this principle is how to enlist the support of the progressive elite without invoking the undying opposition of the conservative elite.

5. *Innovation is accepted faster by the upward bound.*

Sociologists speak of the "upward-mobile" people struggling to rise through the social class system which every society seems to have. The men try to get better, more prestigious jobs; their wives try to move to higher-status neighborhoods. Within the firm, such individuals ordinarily are more likely to accept innovations (provided there is elite support) because they have a higher stake in change than those satisfied with their niche. They will hear an idea and use it. They are not merely trying to please the boss. It is simply that the upward bound have more to gain from change. The problem of innovation posed by this principle is how to feed the idea through the upward-bound people without alienating the complacent ones whose stability is threatened by the change.

6. *Innovation is accepted faster in small packages.*

When Robert Anderson was Secretary of the Treasury, he wanted to induce some change in racial relations. He was unable at that time to make sweeping changes of the kind familiar now, nor did he choose to call his employees together for an emotional speech about black/white brotherhood. He began his campaign by simply directing the painters, over the weekend, to paint over all signs indicating "colored" restrooms. It is true, of course, that there can be heated opposition to even such minor changes. But the strategy of gradualism has much to commend it. One does not try to gulp a steak in one bite. The problem of innovation posed by this principle is how to generate momentum through small changes without arousing suspicion of sneaky, clandestine intentions. The advocates of change suspect "tokenism," while the conservatives fear escalation.

7. *Some persons will accept no innovation at all.*

Here again there is a good sociological term: "alienation." An alienated person feels powerless to influence the decisions which are going to affect his life in a major way. Such a person develops an apathy which barely conceals an essential and profound resentment of his lack of power. The change maker needs to know who (and how numerous) these persons are, and where they are placed. They must be converted, countered, or bypassed. Their greatest danger to the innovation is during the early phases described in the following principle.

8. *For most changes, there is an organizational learning curve.*

When one learns to ride a bicycle, there is a period during which he masters certain subskills (how to take a seat, hold the bars, etc.), but in which he does not actually succeed in riding. Suddenly he then catches on and rolls away, balanced at least for a few feet. The shape of this learning curve (which plots riding skill versus time) is such that it has a series of plateaus. Other learning curves may be gradual, rise indefinitely, suddenly rise and then stop, etc. There are many possible shapes.

Organizations have learning curves (Figure 2.3). These curves have the characteristics already mentioned: they plot skill (or effectiveness) against time. Following the installation of a new method, effectiveness may initially decline below the level previously achieved before it ascends. Put otherwise, the costs may rise initially before they decrease. The result is much like changing one's golf swing. His score may worsen before it improves. The golfer may get fainthearted and revert back before getting through this discouraging period. If he

Organizational Learning Curve

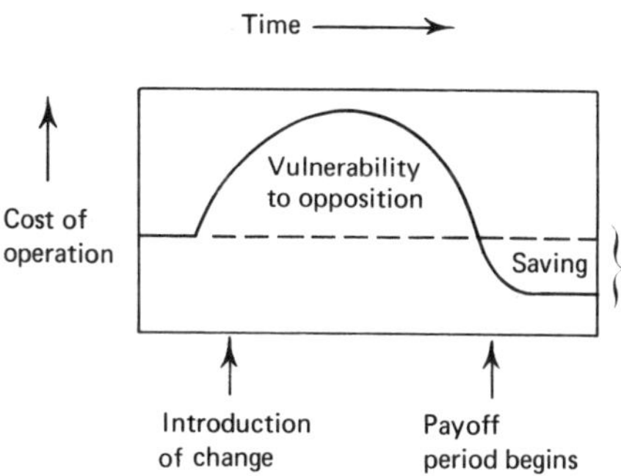

Figure 2.3

does, he may never know how the new swing would have worked. The organization, too, is vulnerable to the conservatives during this initial period. The side effects are felt here. There is stress, tension, uncertainty, and conflict; costs may rise. What is to be done? Planning must be for the learning period and not just for the profitability period—the point on the curve when the organization has turned the corner and the change now becomes profitable. One might plan, for example, to mention the costs during the debate over the change rather than permit them to appear later as an unpleasant surprise.

An Inventory of Principles

The following list summarizes the principles just discussed. They are also diagramed in Figures 2.3 (principle 8) and 2.4 (principles 1 to 7). One way to use such an inventory is to consult it when one is considering introducing a particular change. The list will probably contain several principles which the manager had already thought of using in his planning. He should work these into his plan, and then deliberately reach out for additional ones which he has not used before but which appear potentially useful for the particular planning he is now doing. In this way, the change maker will enlarge his repertoire of tools. The principles discussed were:

1. Hardware changes faster than ideas.
2. Most inventions are made by outsiders.
3. Innovation enters an organization fastest through the top.
4. Innovation enters fastest through the progressive elite.
5. Innovation is accepted faster by the upward bound.
6. Innovation is accepted faster in small packages.
7. Some persons will accept no innovation at all.
8. There is usually an organizational learning curve.

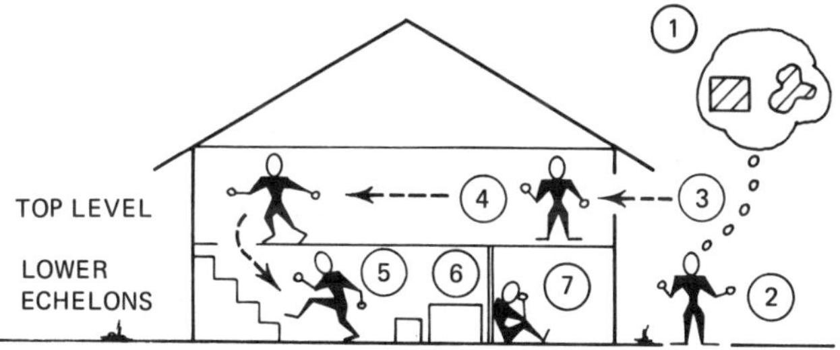

Figure 2.4

Some additional principles, some suggested by the Berelson and Steiner book and some by the observations of others in management, are:

9. Too many changes instituted at one time will slow each other down.

10. If the alienated, conservative, or bureaucratic managers do not destroy an innovation, its side effects may. A side effect of school integration in the South was heavy loss of jobs by black teachers, in some places.

11. Change is accepted faster if it does not appear to violate precedent.

12. People will accept change faster after it has been accepted or advocated by one of their own. The outside expert must be introduced by the hometown "good ol' boy."

13. A highly unified organization is capable of both massive resistance and large-scale rapid change.

14. People want enough change to make their work interesting but not so much as to make it frightening.

15. The more specialists an organization has, the more chances it has for introducing changes which conflict with one another.

16. People will accept change faster if they are first given a chance to talk about it.

17. The chances of change by written directive are near zero.

chapter three

Managing Conflict

Someone gains and someone loses from every major change. Every change is an exchange—whether the change is a new product line, accounting concept, or organization structure, everyone involved will take a look at his personal balance sheet. How will the change affect his:

- influence on company policy?
- income and promotion prospects?
- access to vital data?

The rational model of management assumes every manager, like a good soldier, will accept any eventual decision and determine to make it work. The model presented in this book, however, assumes a limit to this rationality. Hence the change still has to be managed even after the decision to do it has been made.

An additional element which must be assumed is conflict not only with the policy but among the managers. Unless they are walking zombies, the managers will not agree completely either before the decision or after it—companies do not need highly paid managers to make easy decisions. Will this managerial conflict be permitted to run wild, will it be suppressed, or will it be *managed?*

This book is written in troubled times. New suburbs in Washington, D.C., are being constructed with walls to be entered through a guardhouse. They are a good symbol of the age. Who is your favorite villain for the troubles? Too many westerns on TV, the other political party's policies, too many black people, unions, lax parents, strict parents, young people? The truth is, however, that the late sixties and early seventies have been a time of dissent and violence everywhere. Big cities throughout the world have experienced rising crime and disturbances—more likely because they are larger than anyone knows how to manage than because of the variable national political systems. There has been a war some place in the world at all times since World War II. Fantastic arms budgets exist everywhere—not just in the United States.

We used to think that the United States stood a better chance for peace and harmony than most places. But consider now some facts. The United States stands higher on the violence scale than most other Western developed nations. It ranks highest in the per capita ownership of hand guns, and 10,000 people died from gunshot wounds in a year (more deaths than among Americans in Vietnam). The United States is higher in both suicide and murder rates than most. Aside from these rather obvious statistics, the levels of dissent are higher than in recent memory. The most obvious examples are on the American campus. There are also black-white confrontations, Mexican-American demands, an Indian occupation of Alcatraz Island, and recently the women's liberation movement occupied the editorial offices of *McCall's* magazine.

Perhaps the scene for all this is set on television. Millions of viewers are firm fans of the mass mayhem known as professional football. They rise and cheer when the pass receiver is smeared all over the sidelines. True, of course, in Latin America the violence is greater; football can't quite compete for violence with the bullfight, and the soccer crowd is wilder than the football crowd.

The first step toward learning to manage conflict is facing the realities about it. A major reality is that Americans are not, and perhaps usually have not been, a peaceful people. Dissent may tone down this year or next, but it will not go away.

A second reality is that it may not all be bad. Harry Lime, one of the villains in *The Third Man* (the film), had an unconventional opinion of conflicts:

> . . . in Italy for 30 years, under the Borgias, they had warfare, terror, murder and bloodshed, but they produced Michelangelo, Leonardo da Vinci, and the Renaissance. In Switzerland, they had brotherly love . . . 500 years of peace, and what did that produce? The cuckoo clock!

The Renaissance was a great time in the life of man. Perhaps these are now great times (it's hard to tell—we are so close to them); if so, they are not times for timid persons who shrink from conflict.

Quite clearly, an organization or a society does not become productive by becoming violent and authoritarian; if that were so, Paraguay and Bolivia, who have had more dictators than years of history, would be extremely productive. Obviously, the question is how one makes conflict constructive rather than destructive. Sports provide a good example. Consider a golf game between evenly matched adversaries; it brings out the best in both. In football the proper conditions can bring out excellence in effort and performance. One of these key conditions is the coach. After Vince Lombardi died, his players were interviewed and talked about their lives in connection with his. One giant black tackle, summing up what Lombardi meant to him, said, "Lombardi: he's all the man there is."

An athletic game both mobilizes and contains conflict, shaping it into creative and productive effort. Some games provide a better example than others. Football, soccer, and ice hockey do so. In these games it is barely possible to remain a gentleman. I suspect that during debate on big issues, managers are those who find it barely possible to remain gentlemen.

A generation of writings by kindly and well-intentioned behavioral scientists has been stressing the values of cooperation for industry. It is time now to consider the values of conflict.

ASSUMPTIONS ABOUT CONFLICT

These are potentially great times in the United States precisely *because* of the very dissent and divisiveness which trouble us. Nevertheless we run great risks with this divisiveness unless we learn how to manage it. Conflict is always more dangerous than harmony. The payoff, however, for managing conflict may be greater than for maintaining a policy of constant harmony. To be specific:

1. Conflict is normal, not a sign of bad organization.
2. Conflict is often desirable.
3. Conflict is probably inevitable.

If it is normal, often desirable, and in any event probably inevitable, then the manager must learn to manage it rather than fear it or avoid it or ignore it.

Conflict Is Normal

Any change will provoke *real* divisions of interest. They may not just be talked away. A wage increase must come out of somebody's pocket. There is a limit to the number of managers who can be promoted; somebody will be passed by. There is a necessary choice to make, between a new jet airport for New York and somebody's property rights; between more electric power and less pollution. Only a flabby thinker or very young child still believes we can have everything at once. There is no free lunch. Within a corporation, no one really may deny the existence of these conflicts of interest. But it is bad form to talk about them. One admits—there is no way to avoid admitting it—conflict between labor and management. But he would rather not talk about the inherent divisions among some white-collar, professional, and managerial groups. American scientists and engineers, it is known, have had tensions for a long time in the space program. By 1970, for example, tensions between the national academies of these groups had become so great that this "odd couple" had begun to squabble over a variety of things from letterhead design to finance; there was backbiting about each other's professional judgment.[23]

Advocates of easy credit within a sales department historically contend with the financial department. The quality control manager is perennially at odds with the production superintendent. Who does not know about these competitive alignments?

Take a look at the chart of the corporate hierarchy. It resembles, does it not, a system of legal courts? When disputes cannot get resolved at the lower levels, they are passed upstairs for the higher court. How much of the time of the top manager is spent in resolving these "lawsuits" which could not be, or were not, settled at the lower-court level? And does not the parity of power between a line department and one of the major staff departments (say accounting) resemble the check and balance system in which Congress and the federal executive sometimes stand each other off?

Despite the very common occurrence of conflict, some managers become panicky at the first sign of it. It is suggested that they have been brought up to think of the organization in a bureaucratic way. To them, the normal state is the steady state, typified by the harmonious hum of a generator rather than by the grinding gears of an earthmover climbing a steep grade. But most corporations—most of the time—are more like earthmovers than generators. The normal state is tension, conflict, and struggle.

Conflict Is Often Desirable

Don't forget the Renaissance, or the sporting event. In both, we have the example of creative production in the middle of struggle; they faced it and used it in the Renaissance; and in the case of the game, the natural energies people have during conflict are used in a productive way. Add to this the example of our law courts, which operate according to an adversary system. This system, to be sure, has its abuses (we have not denied that conflict has its risks), but no one can think of a substitute for the adversary system.

From industry, we can offer a rather painful piece of evidence: labor grievances. Grievance-handling systems demonstrate the occasional desirability of getting things out in the open, to avoid worse troubles by keeping them hidden.

Even some marriage counselors are beginning to discuss the possibility that a good marriage often requires skill in waging an argument. The creative possibilities of a "knock-down–drag-out" argument have been recently extolled by George Bach, a psychiatrist with excellent credentials in the therapy of sick marriages.

Note what has *not* been said about conflicts:

■ It has not been said that constant conflict is desirable.

■ It has not been said that winning a conflict is always desirable.

■ It has not been recommended to start a fight if things seem too peaceful.

What is always desirable is managing the conflicts that exist, and there are always such conflicts. Management implies a good sense of timing (knowing when a conflict should be encouraged to surface, or whether it should be left alone for a better time). It implies the ability to estimate the relative gains and losses which would result from winning a conflict— sometimes victory is not worth it.

Conflict Is Inevitable

Most major choices in life and in organizations require agonizing choices among alternatives. If one wants to achieve something significant or contend with some major problem, he will take fairly large-scale risks and commit fairly large resources—or else the achievement will be trivial. Where risks are great, someone *should* question them. Conflict helps bring out the facts about risk, like the cross-examination in the courtroom.

A second reason for the inevitability of conflict is the ever-increasing rate of change. The stupendous fact about modern life is that dozens of statistical curves showing social and economic trends—power requirements, waste, crime, taxes, water consumption, paper consumption—are moving almost straight up. The peak is not in sight on some of these trends, and the mind is boggled. It takes a while to get used to the idea of a trillion dollar economy. Since change brings conflict, high change rates intensify it still more.

Yet a third cause of conflict is the rise in ambiguity which every change brings, at least early on during the change. Most of us are uneasy before and during a change; it is all so new, and the dog doesn't want his dish moved from its usual place. The same man who was uneasy about the mini skirt is now indignant about the midi. He thinks he wants to see more stocking, but actually he wants less change, not to speak of the bills.

This uncertainty makes conflict more likely. There is suspicion of intentions. People lower their boiling points, become touchy, interpret one another's behavior as insulting and their intentions as immoral or dangerous. Actions which would earlier have been ignored or accepted become intolerable; the tenth grievance in one week is more dangerous in the factory than the first. A cumulative effect then makes it worse. Fights are more likely to break out in the last minute of a football game than at any other time.

Conflict and Cooperation

In spite of these effects, conflict is not always opposed to cooperation. At any given moment, maybe. In the long run, not necessarily. Conflict need be no more opposed to long-range cooperation than one's left foot, by moving forward, is opposed to the right foot (which must at that moment move backward). The opposed motion makes the larger action, walking, possible; the feet cooperate in the longer run while opposing in the shorter run.

Political parties could not contend if they were not, together, part of a larger political system. The opposing parties in the court of law must be part of the same profession. The opponents in a tennis match are, by fighting, collaborating to produce excellence in performance. Thus we can understand why a grudging respect is sometimes forged during hard-fought negotiations. Conflict often binds men together on deeper emotional levels even while they fight, hammer and tong, on the surface. To wit, at the close of contract negotiations, union and management representatives may unofficially go out for a beer together.

Some conflicts do end without this respect. These are what is called "uncontained conflict" (see Chapter 4); they are exemplified in the student versus administration confrontations which have occurred at places such as San Francisco State.

Conflict management, like big-game hunting, might be considered "the most dangerous game." Whether the term "game" refers to one's adversary or to the "game" of hunting itself, the hazards are still clearly there. It should be played only by the competent. The major difficulty with American and European student uprisings of the past several years has been the amateurism of leadership on both sides. Amateurs almost always lose such conflicts and drag others down with them.

Saul Alinsky, a long-term student and practitioner of urban radicalism, has called the "new far left" a "horribly sick cult," which is moving the United States toward a police state. "Any real revolutionary party would execute them as dangerous counterrevolutionaries . . . . The present radical generation was aborted into a world without radical parents or guides." [24]

The weaknesses of conflict amateurs are particularly dangerous in labor-management negotiations. Professional labor negotiators do not want a corporation's president to conduct its negotiation; he must assume the difficult role of backing the negotiator without being present. This method may produce an anxious time for the president, but it is a necessary way to proceed. Youthful radicals have unfortunately engaged in do-it-yourself political surgery, with the results noted by Alinsky.

Since managers cannot stay out of all conflicts, they must achieve something better than amateur standing in this sport. They must learn well the skills required for conflict management.

1. Those necessary for the detection of conflict
2. Those necessary for the diagnosis of conflict
3. Those involved in the resolution of conflict

Ideally, conflict should be detected as early as possible so that small fires may be kept from combining into large. But the small fire can be more easily misread; a manager who sees conflict where it does not exist will be in a perpetual state of alarm, crying "Wolf!" too much. He can judge with reasonable accuracy, however, if he knows the obvious indicators of trouble—early warning signals. The following list is arranged in rough order of severity:

1. A change in the normal pattern of objection to a new policy or proposed plan (either an increase in objections or a decrease in objections normally raised).

2. A rise in absenteeism (among managers this takes on more subtle forms than among hourly paid workers; e.g., being tied up when a meeting is called, being away on trips constantly, etc.).

3. A persisting issue of abrasive quality—something which is never quite settled and which managers bicker over constantly, but one which really could be settled. Such an issue should be carefully examined to see whether the managers are really in conflict over something else, something more serious.

4. A direct withdrawal of support by some in the power structure.

5. An increase in polarization—i.e., the formation of permanent factions who oppose each other on everything.

6. An increase in quitting or firing for other than performance or economic reasons.

7. A withdrawal by some key people from communication.

A manager must learn to read these signals. The human-relations cases used by schools of business administration contain numerous examples of such conflict signals. By learning to read the signals in the cases, future managers (hopefully) will know how to read them on a later job. Signals are constantly being given all around any manager, however, business-school trained or otherwise; simply beginning to watch will in itself result in a certain sensitivity.

Reading a signal is not sufficient, however. The manager must also react (or not) to it. Persons who react to conflict signals are often much like the student who is assigned a textbook in abnormal psychology for the first time. He begins reacting to neurotic symptoms all around him, whether or not they are really there. This course is unwise and wears people out emotionally. What the student ought to do is learn to look at patients with a cautious concern for their emotional health rather than regard everyone as sick. The reading of a signal does not necessarily demand action, either. If one reacted with action to every signal, he would be putting out a lot of fires which should be left alone, and even imagining some fires which did not exist.

There are other conflict indicators which managers should learn to read, but they require professional help:

DEPTH INTERVIEWING: by interviewing key persons and representative employees in the open-ended manner that marketing people call "depth interviewing," consultants can help the manager take a "reading" of the conflict level and conflict potential within his organization. Depth interviewing is useful unless confidences are breached; if not carefully managed, such a survey can disrupt whatever structure of trust exists and produce a worsening of the very conflicts it was designed to help understand.

POLLING: public-opinion polling is a well-developed art in political life, and there is no reason why it should not be used to understand the conflict potential in a group of managers. Polling differs from depth interviewing in that the survey or poll uses standardized questions and careful sampling methods.

TEST PLANNING: when managers are asked to engage in long-range planning, latent conflicts often emerge regarding their values, their hopes for the organization, and the cliques among them. Interpreting these reactions to the planning process is a professional task as complex, in my judgment, as depth interviewing and polling.

I would suggest that the chief executive of every corporation should receive a periodic "state of the union" report which tells him the organization's temperature. Such reports on labor-management relations are now routine; they are as badly needed to indicate the state of relations among divisions, departments, and managerial personnel.

Diagnosing Conflict

The data possibilities suggested above—the simple early warning indicators and the professional indices of conflict—tell us only a temperature. They do not necessarily tell us *why* the patient has a fever. Deeper investigation is necessary to produce a more complete description of the conflict and, therefrom, to understand it.

Every conflict has several dimensions (e.g., certain people or groups) as well as the issue itself. Describing a conflict requires description in terms of these dimensions:

1. What persons are involved?
2. What interests or factions are involved? This question could be answered in terms of department, geographic area, pressure group, occupational category, or level of the corporation. On the other hand, the conflict may simply be between individuals as suggested in (1).
3. What are the issues? There are surface issues (what is being talked about) and felt issues (beneath the surface but important, and often the more real issue of the two types). Surface and felt issues may, of course, be the same.
4. What are the underlying causes? Fear of losing influence, insecurity about losing work, old antagonisms revived, and even differences in personal work styles, etc.—any of these could conceivably be an underlying cause.

5. What is the extent of the conflict? How far has the fire spread? This question probes escalation and is sufficiently complex that we will discuss it further below.

6. What are the urgencies? Is this particular conflict the most serious one, the one which really demands a manager's attention now more urgently than other conflict and other issues? Will this conflict die out in time if left alone?

The timing of intervention in a conflict often turns on how a manager views its extent. A conflict can escalate in several ways: (1) The issues can become more serious and divisive. (2) The participants can become more numerous (people from everywhere come to a fire). (3) The intensity—how hard people are fighting, what they are willing to "put on the line," etc.— can increase. (4) The positions may harden. One example of this lies in the call for a show-down vote within a group or committee: no matter what the vote, somebody will lose. Such a "win-lose" situation indicates a considerable escalation of the conflict. The early warning indicators discussed above can show a manager how far a conflict has escalated. For example, when persons who normally should communicate stop doing so, the conflict has escalated considerably with respect to intensity, and positions have hardened.

A well-developed conflict will seldom disappear by itself because, like forest fires, conflicts reach out to provide their own fuel. They eventually enter a self-feeding stage at which they can no longer be ignored. They are feeding themselves, for example, when they produce new events which in themselves become divisive issues. A husband (A) who leaves home angrily in the morning and stays away for two days is producing a new event in his marriage. In the interim, his wife's (B's) reaction to his reaction becomes fuel for the flame. A stops communicating with B; B reciprocates, retaliates, raises the ante; A's worst suspicions are confirmed, etc. A hardened position, one which is "self-sealing," develops in short order. An individual in this position has built up his defenses. He has muttered to himself about his grievances for so long that he has a private explanation for everything. Any reasonable argument someone may offer is easily refuted. He has sealed himself in.

The examples just given suggest neurotic or even paranoid behavior (the paranoid state being a classic example of self-sealing). However, words like "immature," "sick," and "neurotic" come to us from the mental-health people. They have been considered useful vocabulary for the clinic and the hospital. Today, however, the usefulness even for psychiatry of the mental-health vocabulary is being questioned by Thomas Szasz,[25] George Albee,[26] and others; if this questioning is valid, we can certainly be even more dubious about the value of such concepts for understanding managerial life.

While conflict may be dangerous, it is very misleading to speak of it as sick or immature. To do so would prevent us from recognizing the creative spark that exists in all conflict. To be creative and innovative, one has to become playful or childlike at times and use his imagination. To object to immaturity or highly emotional behavior is, therefore, to object to the very conditions which can lead to creativity.

A step toward using one's imagination is conventionally viewed as a step away from the rational adult many think managers should be. It is true that the kinds of behavior people show during the escalation of conflict may appear immature or even infantile. The stiff-necked, self-righteous manager who never "blows his cool," however, will probably never learn to manage conflict. Certainly, there are some who indulge themselves in conflict. I have said that conflict is sometimes desirable, but emphatically did *not* say that it is always desirable, did *not* say that there is not a time for peace. Management is not just a disorderly jungle of persons fighting with tooth and claw for their own petty interests. "Social Darwinism," as this image of management is sometimes called, is a silly notion.

We should note one respect in which conflict is never child-like. It is "mature" (if one wishes to use this dubious mental health term) to be realistic, and we suggested above that it is realistic to consider conflict as inevitable. That is simply the way the world is.

Options Open to the Manager

Only after a manager understands the total conflict situation before him should he plan. Most people plan before diagnosing; they simply see tension and react to the signal. Such reactions are very limited, however, because they are only reflexes and not a plan based on diagnosis. Examples of such automatic, reflex actions are:

- Go stop it before it gets worse.
- Talk to the people immediately.
- Have a big meeting and get it out in the open.
- Fire the troublemaker.

Planning is not action but rather the *design* of action. It takes nerve to delay action until a plan exists, but a substantial payoff can result.

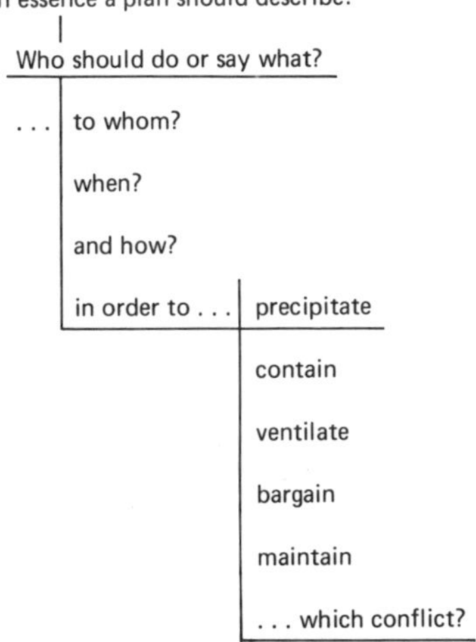

Planning normally opens up the range of options for the manager until finally, when he chooses what seem to be the most optimal responses, he has at least the satisfaction of this wider choice.

Conflict-Management Roles

There are obviously many ways to become involved in a plan of action for coping with conflict. A manager has several possible roles to choose from, some of which are listed below.

1. Go fishing. After going to the trouble of evaluating a conflict and making a plan, the flexible manager should be fully capable of choosing the "do-nothing-at-all" option. There may be too much infection in the body to operate at the moment, and a wise surgeon is conservative at such times. The body has its own defenses; sometimes it is better to let *them* operate.

2. Ombudsman. Some corporations and companies have recently experimented with this Swedish social invention. The Swedish ombudsman is a public representative who helps citizens with grievances against the government. He is a trusted official with no direct authority, only the immense moral power of believing in justice. All doors are open to him.[27]

3. Mediators. We are all familiar with the labor mediator, who must be acceptable to both sides. His role is to get the parties to agree, regardless of his own feelings about the issues. Mediation could be tried within management more often than it is. It may not be done, however, by a line manager in his own division for the simple reason that he cannot maintain the utter neutrality required of mediation.

4. Arbitration. This person must be acceptable to both sides and his judgment accepted by them in advance. In other words, he possesses authority.

5. Participation. One may join a struggle and attempt to swing the balance in a particular direction. This strategy is

sometimes useful in dealing with escalation. One argument for this strategy is discussed below (see Precipitate).

Available Actions

There are several options to consider here, including the do-nothing-at-all role mentioned above. Consider these:

1. Precipitate. When conflicts are between parties grossly unequal in power, the minor may often spend great energy mustering up his courage and his anger. Then when the conflict becomes open, the tension level is so high that the conflict is grossly destructive. This mechanism seems to be one dynamic of revolution. The major power would do better to provoke the outburst earlier and try to settle it then. By waiting for Berkeley students to become bitter, the administration (the state? the university?) helped to create a permanent revolutionary cadre.

2. Contain. When conflicts are not settled, the issues often enlarge. The simplest example of containment is prompt settlement. However, containment refers primarily to a permanent set of ground rules for identifying and settling disputes. A jurisprudence for corporations should be created such that not only workers with grievances but managers and professionals have a pattern of communication within which to settle their complaints and express conflicts. Without such containment procedures, we may see more professional and even managerial unions within the decade. However, containment is not a union-busting strategy; it is part of conflict management.

3. Ventilate. This is a simpler action and is based on the premise that the conflicting parties primarily need the chance to express their feelings.

4. Bargain. When the parties are of approximately equal power, formal or informal bargaining can take place. In all such bargaining, the issue must be complex; that is, there must be some points on which horse trading can be done.

(Issue A is traded for issue B.) If the entire conflict is a simple win-lose issue, bargaining is almost impossible. A large part of the following chapter is devoted to bargaining.

5. Maintain. A tension level may be deliberately maintained, with no attempt to resolve the conflict for the time being. This differs from doing nothing at all in that the conflict manager has decided that the tension level is in the interests of the organization, and if it appears to decline, he will whip it up again. This is the game played by executives who want different divisions to compete and "whiplash" them by calling one another's achievements to their general attention. But it is a game played only by very advanced professionals and is dangerous even there. Look what happened to G.E. in the price-fixing debacle, in which one interpretation was that excessive competition among managers had been encouraged by the top executives.

chapter four

The Diplomacy of Management

Corporations are now so large that they have been compared to national states. General Motors contributes enough in federal corporate taxes to support the entire field of health research, according to Richard Barber,[18] who further says, "General Motors—to take just one example—is a political 'state' except to those who are interested in formalities." Much recent concern has been voiced over how to make such giants serve the public interest. One may also question whether they even serve their own individual interests.

Size is not the only factor that causes difficulty in governance, but certainly it is one which is illustrated in all large institutions, not just corporations. Consider the 40,000 students on the campus of a typical large state university in America, or the vastly larger campus populations of some European universities. No one knows how to govern this large a number of critically minded, inventive, and restless single youth, nor is there any known model for persuading them to govern themselves.

The sheer size of corporations has produced new management problems, and regarding them as states may suggest useful new concepts and techniques. Among more useful elements of "statecraft" is diplomacy. The reader may complain: "Heaven help us if we have to have a corporate State Department!" Such, however, is not my suggestion. We will simply explore the idea of diplomacy.

Forget the image that diplomats are persons of tact. There was a time when diplomats wore morning coats, spoke amiably without saying much, and wrote endless reports home. But this image is too limited and in any event distracts us from understanding the mission and methods of diplomacy. One central task of diplomacy is to resolve international tensions in a productive manner. This chapter substitutes for "international" such phrases as "intergroup," "interdivision," and "interdepartment." It applies some of the concepts of diplomacy and finds that some have long been used in corporations—for example, in labor relations; its proposal, therefore, is to use more widely an expertise that already exists.

**The Growing
Limitations upon Authority**

Chapter 3 closed by discussing the exposure of raw conflicts and the consideration of alternative strategies which facilitate conflict management. Let us assume an urgent situation in which a raw conflict suddenly develops beyond the point of no return and cannot be swept under a rug. It might be a board fight, a fight between major divisions, or even a dispute across departmental lines (perhaps between younger and older managers). Some might argue for resolution of the conflict simply by appeal upward into the hierarchy. After all, this argument would go, the corporation itself is designed as a pyramid in which managers report to common bosses, who in return report to their common chieftains, etc. in the fashion of a court system. The chain of command is designed to resolve conflicts as well as to make noncontroversial decisions, accept reports, and monitor performance. But this rational authority design is not always usable and has become increasingly inadequate as a conflict-management model. This inadequacy is difficult for anyone outside a particular organization to comprehend. The general public, for example, is quite baffled as to why universities do not exercise more authority over students and even professors. Why can't cities stop crime? Why can't churches simply direct people to be moral?

Later in this chapter we will discuss the uses of authority in a corporation as one among several techniques useful in conflict resolution; here suffice it to say that several factors have reduced the feasibility of authority as the primary tool.

Open-ended *versus* Organized Conflict

The use of authority over younger generations has been a matter of concern. Consider two examples from Dartmouth College in 1969. In the one, conflict was met with authoritarian tactics, and in the other it was not. In the spring, strong attacks were made on administration policy by two large bands of students. The two bands differed in style of attack, and the administration's response differed accordingly.

One attack, conducted by a coalition of several radical groups (notably the SDS—Students for a Democratic Society) demanded abolition of military training and other moves which would express rejection of the war in Vietnam. These students occupied an administration building by force, carried out at least one protesting official. The other attack, conducted by the "Afro-American Society," came in the form of a list of written demands. These eighteen demands focused around increasing the number of black students on campus (to a "quota" of 10 percent). No buildings were occupied, but the demands were interpreted as menacing in tone if not directly threatening or insulting.

In response to those who occupied the building, Dartmouth College requested the court to issue an injunction to leave the property. The enforcement of such injunctions then lay in the hands of the New Hampshire State Police, whose training had been carefully prepared some time previously. They arrived well before the injunction deadline, which had been delibertately set to permit the occupiers to discuss their response to it. The deadline came in the middle of the night. When the occupiers did not leave, the police forced the door and carried the demonstrators out. No guns were on hand. There were few, if any, blows, although the scene had a violent atmosphere since much of the campus had gathered to watch the demonstrators being forced into a large police van (within which they yelled and beat the sides in indignation and excitement). The demonstrators were tried in court and, for the most part, sentenced to a month in jail. With these demonstrators there was no negotiation, and the response could be termed conflict resolution by overwhelming force.

The Afro-Americans, by contrast, occupied no buildings. Following receipt of their demands, the college appointed a negotiating committee which met with Afro representatives at great length. The negotiations were tense and harassing. Most of the demands were met, although for one year following the immediate resolution, it was necessary that a "Committee on Equal Opportunity" meet weekly to review and cope with the various tensions which would arise from time to time and might cause the agreement to break down.

These two styles of conflict resolution are found not just in universities but in a variety of institutions:

■ *Open-ended* conflict, as in the building occupation; guerrilla warfare; rioting; the resistance of a captive population to an occupying army; and labor-management conflict in the early days of American union history.

■ *Organized* conflict, as in the Afro-American demands; the takeover of stock in a corporation raid; and labor-management conflict in more recent union history.

There are many models for conflict resolution. Their applications for resolving tensions among managers and other groups (among whom, in theory, there *is* no conflict!) will be this chapter's prime concern.

Among the kinds of factions likely to be involved in intra-corporation conflict are:

■ scientists versus line managers

■ top versus middle management

■ old-timers versus newcomers among the managers

■ executives in a newly acquired corporation versus the parent corporate executives

■ generalists versus staff specialists as a group

■ members of a task force versus established division managers

■ sales versus manufacturing

■ quality control versus manufacturing

■ personnel administration versus line management

and these struggles are always happening. In Chapter 3 I suggested that conflict is normal, often desirable, and in any event, inevitable. Change increases the frequency, intensity, and dangers of conflict. As the rate of change in society and in most corporations is itself increasing, we may confidently expect conflict within corporations to increase.

The aims of corporate diplomacy are to prevent or settle all such conflicts—or manage them. They are a source of energy (who doesn't have more energy when he gets angry?) and therefore of productive work. Intracorporate struggles may be compared to the fires of a nuclear reactor; we have to learn to build one, operate it, control its accidents. Energy, unmanaged, is dangerous.

OPEN-ENDED CONFLICTS IN THE CORPORATION

Some of these struggles are fought over issues and under ground rules which are vague. They are fought behind the walls of the executive suite through which filter only the muted sounds of shouts and blows to feed the gossip mill of the coffee break. Someone once compared the executive suite to a dog fight under a blanket.

The first two characteristics of open-ended conflict have already been mentioned: the lack of clear-cut issues and of ground rules. As the conflict escalates, other features appear. A full list of characteristics follows:

1. Goals and issues are unclear or in dispute.
2. Ground rules for defining and settling the dispute are not agreed upon (e.g., there's no grievance procedure).
3. Many parties are involved rather than one or two clearly designated spokesmen.
4. The participants or negotiators are amateurs without experience in or knowledge of corporate diplomacy.
5. Violence (to persons or property) and extreme illegal action become possible.
6. The mass media eventually become involved and are used by both sides.
7. There is acrimony throughout, and even after the conflict ends, some bitterness usually remains.

Goals and Issues in Open-ended Conflict

The issues are often vague and concerned with such nonnegotiable matters as style. When the young in America are quarreling with the *style* of something called the "Establishment" or "Middle America," there is almost nothing specific which can be debated. At Dartmouth College, it was possible to negotiate with the Afro-Americans because the issues were specific. The building occupiers *also* presented demands; but it was obvious that their demands would, when granted, be succeeded by new demands; no negotiation could work.

Some conflicting factions in the corporation will present a similar problem. The research men may dislike the *style* of the bureaucrat. The production men just do not think like the media men; this is an interesting diversity in style, but when it becomes a conflict, two such factions have much in the way of a "hidden agenda" which is difficult to discuss, impossible to resolve.

Ground Rules in Open-ended Conflict

There are no ground rules, agreed on by both sides, for settling such conflicts. In part, this is because neither side may recognize or even want to admit that it is engaged in conflict. The norm in so many corporations—especially those with a bureaucratic tradition—is to get along well with people, to cooperate, to coordinate. No one may want to go to a potential mediator, and especially not to his boss, and say, "I just can't seem to settle my dispute with X; I need help." Still less do cliques want to admit they are cliques. But when foremen meet, they grouse. And while the grousing may be harmless venting off of steam, if their situation becomes bad enough and they convince one another of this, it will eventually occur to them to set up some kind of collective defense. They may also unionize.

Such *ground rules* are agreements between the two sides that disputes will be settled in a certain way. To agree on such rules, the parties must agree that (1) a conflict exists or potentially exists; (2) a measure of trust exists even so; (3) the conflict should be controlled; (4) the means of control and/or resolution will be roughly spelled out; and (5) it is in the interest of all parties to settle the conflict in such a manner.

A minimum amount of trust must exist before any negotiation can be undertaken. Sometimes days or years in international diplomacy are spent merely in trust building and maneuvering; only afterward is progress made. Diplomacy and trust building can be accomplished much more easily and rapidly within a corporate setting than in the international.

Agreement that a conflict should be ended is not always possible. At Dartmouth College, it was not in the interest of the chronic radicals to end the conflict, and any negotiation with them would have proved futile. The Afro-Americans, however, had no interest in a perpetual war on the Establishment, and a settlement was possible. In a corporation, it is generally of mutual value to end a conflict, and there is thus some hope of moving a conflict from open-ended to organized status.

The Many Parties Involved

Few conflicts are limited to just two parties. For example, it is almost impossible to negotiate with the extreme left-wing "group" in a college. It is a loose coalition of people who will rarely unite behind one or two leaders. (If they ever did, it would be possible to move the conflict to an organized basis.) Open-ended conflict is usually waged between parties at least one of whom has no hierarchy. Thus, no agreement would be binding even if it were reached. The situation is rather like that which sometimes occurs in labor relations when an agreement reached at the bargaining table is subsequently repudiated by either management or the union's members.

Intracorporation factions can have spokesmen only if they admit that a conflict exists. But merely becoming a spokesman can put that person in a most difficult position. For example, if all an organization's newly hired college graduates felt that they had a raw deal, they would probably choose a spokesman to confront the management because new employees have little to lose. Older employees in a similar position, however, have much to lose and would be unlikely to choose a spokesman because he would be placed in a very precarious position or would at least feel that he was. Older employees would probably choose to fight an underground battle over the issue.

Amateurism

Amateurism is often a problem for all parties in an open-ended conflict. Hospitals, for example, were ill-prepared for the sudden onset of union organizing activity which appeared in the sixties. Hospital managers did not always have the expertise to manage these conflicts and quickly lost control not only of the manpower situation but of hospital costs in general. College administrators were likewise absolutely unprepared for the radical onslaught of the sixties. The open-ended conflicts may be subsiding, but they have never, for the most part, been resolved or translated into organized conflicts. The students in such conflicts, of course, are always amateurs, and it is astonishing that America has not experienced more killing and burning by youth groups. We have seen the destructive effects of the Red Guards in China, of their equivalent in France, of students in Latin American universities.

Within a corporation, conflicts are fought by amateurs in the sense that the antagonists lack skill and background for their actions. In Chapter 5 I will discuss the effect of this amateurism in terms of emotional stress.

Violence, Damage, Apathy

Open-ended conflict poses a greater likelihood (at the point of maximum escalation, of course) of violence to people, property, or the corporate image and unity. Violence is more likely to be directed toward the organization than to people and things. Engineers are unlikely to pour sand into the machinery, but they may quit, or else—the most likely outcome —subside into the apathy which has often been judged the outstanding characteristic of our age. Apathy should not be seen as characteristic of aging employees per se; rather, it is probably the result of losing too many battles, of being bypassed for promotion, and of lacking the emotional capacity to face the conflicts of age.

The Mass Media

A conflict must escalate quite substantially before it is noticed by the mass media. I remember a corporation president who wanted to move his home office to another city. He knew that the board of directors would never agree, but he nevertheless set the wheels in motion for the move; he reasoned that a fait accompli would settle the matter, and the board would have to go along. The board did not. He made the issue one of his presidency itself; they fired him. The press heard of it, interviewed him, and got his version. One wonders what effect this publicity ultimately had on the corporation's stock.

We may be coming, however, to an era in which the rise of *public-interest* law firms and other organized critics of corporations may force more publicity into areas of corporate life which were previously immune. In that case the manager who cannot manage his relations with the media may have great difficulties. In open-ended conflict, the media's role (in the eyes of its critics) is generally to confuse issues and aggravate the conflict. Rioters learn to pose before TV cameras. Youthful radical leaders, interviewed by the national press, become public figures; who can resist that siren song? The weaker party to a conflict, seeking wider public support and recruits to its cause, will often try to involve the media. A newspaper reporter can often interview a dissident and aggrieved employee or manager. Managers siding with the corporation, however, are often reluctant to talk to the press. Future types of manager and working styles may well change this condition.

Residual Bitterness

The long-range costs of open-ended conflicts can be very great. When momentary peace comes to a corporation or division which has not managed its conflicts, there is no real restoration of relationships. An offending party may be fired; a group of engineers may quit and form their own corporation; several old persons may accept early retirement; whatever the resolution, it does not result in much good feeling.

The opposing parties in "campus wars," which have been fought in this manner, build up a store of ill will which endures for long periods. On some such campuses, it is as if the air is poisoned. Students walk about in a quiet state of bitterness; professors are in a state of bewilderment; there is a profound loss of confidence. This social condition is too subtle for a legislature, an alumni body, or the general public to understand. Regardless of whether such campuses had ever developed any real unity, they no longer possess much strength and purpose.

In order that this not happen to a corporation, it can adopt one of three general strategies: (1) develop a conflict strategy; (2) move conflicts, when they do arise, into an organized style of conflict resolution; (3) adopt a bureaucratic form of organization in which disputes can be largely prevented by rule making in advance (e.g., a bureaucratic organization has few salary quarrels because it makes very complete rules in advance).

ORGANIZED PATTERNS
FOR RESOLVING CONFLICT

When the parties to a conflict have accepted the necessity for some kind of ground rules for resolving it, it becomes possible to manage the conflict. Such a conflict then becomes organized, and it contrasts with open-ended conflict at almost every point. What patterns exist for managing conflicts?

Resolution by Authority

The first and most familiar model for conflict resolution is the direct use of authority. A certain amount of the boss's decision making is not simply choosing among rational alternatives, as textbooks on decision making put it, but choosing among contending parties. How much of the wear and tear of executive life is due to the strains of this kind of decision making? Perhaps it is overused. At any rate, the conditions necessary for its appropriate use are not always present.

One of these conditions would seem to be a unitary issue. If the issue is where to put a plant, and that alone, then the general manager may find he can readily and appropriately resolve it. However, if faction A (which says Hawaii) and faction B (which says Bimini) are at loggerheads not only on this issue, but on a number of other issues, then the general manager is not dealing with a unitary issue. Something more than the exercise of authority is required.

This requirement is related to a second condition. Authority is perhaps better considered a force in being than an active power. Military forces in constant war are not being permitted to do their job, which is to *keep* the peace. If courts are used too often, they become clogged (as at the present time), and the law breaks down. So also with the corporate executive. His authority if never used may disappear; but if frequently used, it can paralyze the organization in many ways. Thus, the condition for the appropriate use of authority in settling a particular dispute is that it has not been used recently.

A third condition is that the person in authority shall understand the issue. In corporations with many different staff specialties, it is all too possible that they may be debating a technical matter which the person in authority does not understand.

A fourth condition is that the parties and the person in authority should be able to meet face-to-face. There seems no substitute for the direct exchange. It is impossible to imagine serious conflicts being resolved by mail.

Mediation

The boss is sometimes more useful in conflict management if he is neutral. His third-party status is then a useful feature in resolving conflict. Richard Walton has pointed out many ways in which one can be useful in resolving conflicts, simply by being a third party.[28] However, power may get in the way of open discussion and full solution.

The problem is that the sole interest of the mediator is conflict settlement. This means he has no interest in settling the dispute in one direction rather than the other (unlike the boss, who tries to resolve it in the best direction). Thus his help can be accepted in the interests of peace without any implication that one side really had a better case than the other. The mediator does not settle a dispute; he helps the people settle it. This means they do not have to admit their inadequacies, as it would sometimes seem when they have to go to the boss. Among the conditions required for mediation is the agreement by both sides to communicate with the mediator. They do not have to agree in advance (as with the authoritative arbitration) to abide by his solutions.

Mediators do not have to know much, it would seem, about the technical aspects of a conflict. They need to know enough to make suggestions about possible settlements, but not enough to evaluate the moral, economic, and other values involved in each side's position. The personnel and production departments, for example, could ask the marketing man to settle a dispute.

The boss of two factions can never be mediator. When he stops evaluating both positions, he stops being a boss.

Ombudsman

There is currently an interest in still another model of conflict resolution—the ombudsman. Consideration is being given to appointing ombudsmen in both public affairs and in corporations.[27] An ombudsman resembles both patterns just described. For example, he will not accept a problem if he does not think the person has a justified cause, and in this respect he evalutes issues, as does the boss. However, when he accepts a case (somewhat like an attorney would), he attempts to get the person complained against to settle it; he has no authority at this point, relying only on persuasion. Thus he resembles the mediator. If he cannot get the conflict settled by informal, behind-the-scene methods, he bows out of it altogether.

The ombudsman is suited for problems in which the offended party has far less power than the other. He adds his moral weight of concern to the lesser party, compelling the heavier party to listen. In Scandinavia, he is an advocate of the underdog, especially of the individual citizen who is, or feels, abused by the government.

Collective Bargaining

When a conflict has escalated, when the parties have crystallized themselves into rather definite factions, when they are roughly similar in power—under these conditions, we cannot be sure whether the conflict has gone beyond appropriate solution by the above three models. It is conceivable that a modified form of *collective bargaining* is the only remaining model for conflict resolution at this point. In fact, one wonders if some interminable business conferences, which seem to make little sense to the participants, are not actually disguised or poorly run bargaining sessions.

We are not saying that there should be a union of middle managers, senior employees, scientists—or whatever the faction is. For one thing, we are talking about conflicts among the managers and professionals, rather than between management and labor. Managers and professionals do not draw up formal contracts with one another; but they do make policies, work out procedures, choose priorities, and make other decisions which are of joint interest to one another.

They have groups of issues and feelings which ought to be aired. John Coggswell, at AT&T, has devised and used a way of helping different corporate groups (divisions, departments, etc.) engage in organized confrontation and comparison of their views of one another, for the sake of getting their cards on the table, releasing tension, and arriving at better agreements on how they are to operate together.

Recognition of these social forces should not be delayed further in corporations. It has not been over two decades since it was common to doubt that there would ever be white-collar unions of engineers, pilots, professors, physicians, nurses, and teachers; we have them all today, even though we may have other names for these organizations.

Collective bargaining on the managerial levels of the corporation contrasts with open-ended conflict, as in the other models of authority, mediation, and ombudsman, in regard to several points:

1. The goals and negotiable issues are stated (they are not, in open-ended conflict).

2. Ground rules are agreed on, for settling the dispute. These rules would normally include provision for nose-to-nose hammering out of an agreement.

3. The factions each designate specific spokesmen.

4. These spokesmen should be experienced negotiators, perhaps even attorneys or labor-relations men.

5. Extreme illegal actions and underground sabotage of one another's operations, which are possible with open-ended conflict, are unlikely in organized conflict.

6. Both sides rigidly exclude publicity.

7. While there may be acrimony during the conflict, it is usually dissipated by the end of negotiation.

CORPORATE DIPLOMACY

Now we move beyond conflict resolution to the problem of framing a total policy for conflict management—i.e., the arts and disciplines of diplomacy. Corporate diplomacy is not statecraft, but the lessons of statecraft are instructive. In fact, Sir Harold Nicolson,[29] who writes from long experience in statecraft, sees diplomacy as "an essential element in any reasonable relation between man and man."

Administrative theory is rich in concepts, and justification must be offered for new ones. The following are reasons we should reach beyond the traditional concepts of human relations into the less familiar and new area of statecraft:

1. The rise of multinational firms has produced communication problems and conflict hazards of a new order.

2. The very size of corporations makes necessary new conceptions of organization.

3. Even within corporations no larger than sales of a million a year, new problems have arisen because of the proliferation of new types of staff services and technical specialties.

4. The equalization of literacy and education among different levels of management (certainly in the United States, we have not commonly had the educated manager supervising the illiterate worker for some decades) renders the mistakes of higher management more visible and makes arbitrary authority look ridiculous.

Anthony Jay [30] argues that history teaches as much about management as business cases do. This is not merely because large national states are Machiavellian, just as corporations in some degree, but more fundamentally because management deals with vast complexities (people, things, dollars), just as governments do.

In general, corporate diplomacy refers to the arts and disciplines which govern relations among people or divisions of roughly equal power. It is useful whenever a problem cannot or should not be resolved by directive or routine report. Its continual exercise prevents the kinds of crises discussed in earlier pages (page 69). In this area, practice has far outgrown theory. As this practice has not been codified, one can report only a few sample illustrations.

The most obvious examples of a problem demanding corporate diplomacy are probably in corporate mergers. Company A acquires company B, let us say. It is larger than B and has the markets B does not, but lacks the production and technical expertise of B. While they both need each other, the language and legal arrangements suggest B is the "inferior" partner, and this implication is among the early problems of diplomacy faced by the executives of A and B.

The executives of A/B face a problem of integrating B into the larger system without ruining the assets which were purchased. If the best of B's former key people either leave or remain but do not contribute, the entire merger operation may ultimately fail with respect to its initial goals. The integration of two organizations is delicate and in many ways must be gradual. The labor relations departments, for example, might be kept totally separate for several years. The plan for integration demands far more subtle judgments than the original appraisal which produced the merger; it requires diplomatic planning.

The closing and subsequent moving of a manufacturing plant provides another example. A premature announcement of the closing will generate local political pressures. A careless announcement will generate ill will on the part of the employees who, it is hoped by the company, will want to move to the new locale. The move and its announcement must also be planned in keeping with the needs of customers who may be lost if they suspect that future delivery schedules will be disrupted or that their needs will no longer be given priority.

Or consider how a company with overseas branches determines what proportion of nationals will be taken into a branch's group. A large oil company, for example, may learn that its American executives in a North African oil-producing country are causing difficulties simply because they are not nationals. It, therefore, conceives a plan for gradually replacing those Americans with North African nationals.

These examples suggest problems in public relations, manpower management, labor relations, business-government relations, and management development. They branch into a dozen different specialized staff functions; indeed, this indicates a very important aspect of corporate diplomacy—it is exceedingly broad.

We should also observe that, in two of the examples, the diplomatic process is a very long-term one which must be planned and carried out over a period of years. However, and this is the third point well made in the plant-closing example, the diplomatic process may need to be applied to a short-range or crisis situation.

The variety of functions involved in corporate diplomacy is so great that they could not be assigned to a particular department in every company. It should not be considered a new staff specialty but rather a function of general management. Accordingly it would be irrelevant to list the techniques of corporate diplomacy. General managers do not need to cultivate any new sets of skills which were not required before. They need only develop a deeper appreciation of the nature of organizations.

The Future of Authority

Corporations with far-flung divisions must cope with the tendency of those divisions to become self-sufficient "cultures," with strong needs to be autonomous and to resist outside influence. This problem is also faced by corporations whose operations are located in one place but whose departments have become "little empires." Both aspects of this are becoming worse:

- The rise in multinational, worldwide firms has increased problems of integration and coordination.
- The continuing proliferation of staff functions has increased the difficulties of centralized authority.

Both aspects require diplomatic handling.

At this point we should consider a question which may have occurred to the reader: why won't the traditional structure of authority eventually solve these problems? I do not need to repeat the difficulties of decentralization through which many American corporations suffered in the early days of hope regarding the virtues of granting greater autonomy to every unit.

The issue of delegating versus not delegating authority is far too simplistic an issue here. Diplomacy is needed whether authority is held tightly or not; but in general, the concept of corporate diplomacy is easier to understand when the limitations of authority are recognized.

The company, like a government or any other giant institution, cannot enforce every directive. It cannot monitor every operation. It issues every policy statement in an atmosphere of hope that it essentially will be followed. The limitations of authority on the particular company, government, or institution may be narrow or broad, but they are assuredly there. Herbert Simon [31] termed this fact of life the "zone of acceptance." Every employee has a zone of actions within which he will accept a direct command, and outside of which he will not. He will accept directions within the time zone of nine to five, but hourly paid workers will often reserve the right to decide whether they will engage in work after five, even at the overtime rate. Within the limited zone of acceptance, authority is a tool, if not the only tool. Outside that zone, when dealing with divisions and departments, a management's tools must include corporate diplomacy if it is to manage successfully.

Nor is corporate diplomacy limited to the central management of a corporation. The outlying divisions and specialized departments have their own diplomatic plans, representatives, and procedures. Terms like communication, persuasion, and even salesmanship are used to refer to the relations among such units. Such terms are often used too narrowly, leading us to underestimate grossly the long-range character and broad scope of corporate diplomacy's greatest difficulty. This problem is, briefly, that as authority declines, diplomatic talent must increase. The long-run trend is toward increasing restraint on the use of authority. This trend has not resulted from ideological objection to it (as eloquently voiced, for example, by Likert [32] and McGregor [33]), but rather the cause is that authority is becoming increasingly impractical for reasons inherent in organizational structure.

The Future of Negotiation

There is, perhaps, one technique which can be named. It is the central skill involved in collective bargaining. Negotiation is that interchange between equals which results in agreements on plans of action and on procedures.* After two units have successfully negotiated, there is a decrease in tension between them and an increase in interchange of ideas and benefits. Much of the time the relation between an outlying unit and its central office is better negotiated than commanded. In the end, of course, the central office has authority at its command; and both parties know that, in some respects, their powers are

---

* See Schelling,[34] Chapter 2, for an explanation of how bargaining sometimes equalizes unequals.

unequal. But during the negotiations, the man-to-man communication preserves their dignity and that of the divisions they represent. Negotiation is possible among sovereign states, even though one may possess a hundred times the power of the other. In this respect, statecraft is often more human than ordinary social relations.

What happens during negotiation is a trade-off of benefits and advantages. This is not to say that, during any one negotiation, department A will not be asked to do something for department B unless a price is paid. It is true, however, that over a long series of negotiations, a price is always paid. This simply states the obvious. What is less obvious is that, in a corporation's design, each department must be given counters which it can trade off, or it will not be able to command the necessary collaboration and attention from those with whom it must deal. I have never met an organizational theorist who laid out a corporate structure with this logrolling in mind.

The purpose of corporate diplomacy in all such negotiations should be the overall benefit of the corporation and, in turn, of the larger societies it serves. But it is too much to expect that the piety of "greater good for the corporation" or "for society" will be sufficient to resolve most nitty-gritty issues between divisions or departments. In a drug-manufacturing corporation, for example, is it better for the production department to make less vaccine in order to reduce pollution? These are the kinds of issues usually negotiated rather than simply whether production should go up or down.

Diplomacy as Necessity

Diplomacy is rational interaction among irrational units. It is an impossible task which is necessary. The size of some corporate giants and their multinational character also look impossible, yet they are functioning anyway! Theory must, therefore, catch up with practice.

Kenneth Boulding [35] has marveled at the genius implicit in some of the "organizational revolutions" which have taken place. Coordinating the 20,000 corporations involved in making equipment for the lunar landing was an act of organizational genius. We may not yet know how this coordination was accomplished, but we had better learn. Many areas of common life have deteriorated because of the lack of managerial skill. We need only note:

- the governance of cities
- the management of hospitals and medical care
- university governance
- the management of such runaway processes as pollution and population

The point is not that the particular men who managed the lunar shot are themselves able to solve these problems in common life. Rather, it is suggested (even desperately hoped) that discernible, useful principles can be found in their work. Such principles would guide us in what seems to be an unmapped swamp, a bog, even a quicksand: the management of public services.

Even within the corporation, is the expertise of corporate diplomacy sufficient? Why are there interminable meetings on high levels which do not really settle anything in some corporations? Why are there general managers who feel pulled in all directions by decision making, while the staff managers sometimes boil in frustration, waiting for action? Are there not some areas of corporate life presenting a surface apathy which conceals dangerous potential disruption beneath? Preventative management of conflict, which is to say corporate diplomacy, looks for these facts rather than avoiding them.

chapter five

Eu-stress

The risk taker, by definition, lives dangerously—more so than his bureaucrat counterpart, "Mr. Safe." He not only expects to be judged by results; he actually asks for trouble by being a *change seeker;* he must, then, of necessity, be a conflict manager. Eventually he must become a collective bargainer and negotiator, able to work himself out of the political troubles his risk taking has gotten him into!

It is high time, some readers may insist, to consider whether risk taking is an emotionally healthy way of life. This chapter answers this question from two perspectives:

■ First, the conventional mental-health answer: that stress is a medical and psychological "problem."

■ Second, a more recent view that stress is the spice of managerial life—a psychological "benefit."

The scientific popularity of the term "stress" dates back to the work of a medical genius, Hans Selye.[36] Selye documented the occurrence in rats of a set of physical effects resulting from prolonged exposure to extremes of heat, cold, etc., which he called the "general adaptation syndrome." This syndrome, found only in rats who died young and of *no discoverable disease* except the prolonged exposure to stressful situations in the laboratory, was interpreted to be the result of that stress.

In extending the concept of general adaptation syndrome to humans, Selye was ambitiously seeking a general rationale for just plain being sick and for the wear and tear of life. Every patient intuitively knows this experience—he is miserable, restricted in what he can do. He knows also what it means to have a "hard life," and suspects a connection between having a hard life and getting sick. The pre-Selye medical diagnostician looked for signs of underlying disease, the basic cause. Such diagnosticians were not trained to give much attention to just plain being sick. In contrast, Selye directed his research attention to just being sick, taking it seriously enough to investigate its general underlying mechanism. What he and the many investigators who have followed his lead uncovered is worth thinking about for managers who consider that they have a hard life or suffer stress.

We'll skip the physiology here but instead use an analogy which portrays it just about as well. The general adaptation syndrome (just being sick) develops from a sequence of events in the sick patient which might be compared to a fire:

1. There is an alarm period; bells ring and the "physiological firemen" rush to the engines, moving to the fire as rapidly as possible. The patient may know he is coming down with something, may be unusually active or excited at this point.

2. There is a fire-fighting period; the firemen are fighting

the disease, whatever it is, and other normal activities are suspended to give them room and resources. The patient is often feverish and stays abed. This is the acute phase, the crisis.

3. The fire goes out; the trucks move slowly, clanging back to the station. The patient enters a recovery period in which he is not yet back to normal and must rest, but is no longer in a crisis.

Selye's theory has inspired heavy volumes of research since his initial writing. It is among the most influential medical thinking of this century. However, not all scientists agree with its importance, and he won't ever win a Nobel prize—the traditional medical glamor lies in research which analyzes specific diseases rather than formulates general theory. His work also experiences other difficulties when extended to the human level. One is determining precisely what constitutes stress. Stress cannot be defined merely as a simply physical stimulus, except in very exceptional circumstances (such as prolonged cold or hunger). A wound received in battle might be thought a physical stress. But such a physical stimulus is felt as a stress in relation to its context. Thus the victim may not even feel the wound during the battle; on noticing it afterwards, he faints. Pain intolerable to one man may hardly be noticed by another; professional athletic skill consists, in part, of acquiring the ability to ignore pain.

Hence, Selye's physiological method of research cannot be sufficient for humans, who are not automatons and thus require research techniques of a psychophysiological nature. There has been much psychological research in stress, but psychologists are by no means agreed that it is a useful concept. In spite of this, the concept of stress—provided we define it carefully for each situation we want to discuss—appears essential to understanding the working life of executives. Managing the intricate and rapid processes of change in a large corporation is almost more than some managers can take. Is this fact due to a limited tolerance for stress? Should managers with limited stress tolerance be put in easier jobs? Should the rate of change (as in mergers, for example) be held down to tolerable levels?

Toffler [17] cites a piece of research by Thomas Holmes and Richard Rahe [37] in which they use a questionnaire to determine the amount and type of change an individual has experienced in a given span of time. The rate of change for individuals is quantified on a point scale in which the death of one's spouse is rated at 100 points, changing jobs at 20 points, etc. Holmes and Rahe then questioned people, rated them on their amount of life change, and found this result: those with high life-change point scores were far more likely to be ill in the months following the questionnaire. The questionnaire thus predicted the incidence of physical illness.

Toffler interprets this research as confirmation of his future-shock hypothesis. Toffler's thinking resembles Selye's except Toffler relates his thinking to broad economic, political, social, and technical change in a way that Selye did not. Toffler said that there are:

> . . . discoverable limits to the amount of change that the human organism can absorb, and that by endlessly accelerating change without first determining these limits, we may submit masses of men to demands they simply cannot tolerate. We run the high risk of throwing them into that peculiar state that I have called future shock [p. 290].[17]

The implication of this concept (and of the Holmes and Rahe study) is at first glance clear: slow down; don't impose too much change on people; they will get sick, react irrationally (even violently), and so on.

Another piece of evidence comes from the work of Rubin [38] who has shown that those countries whose rate of economic progress has been greatest—particularly the United States and Japan—are also those which record the highest *external* and *internal* violence rates. We know that external violence is the act of killing, either suicide or murder; and it is higher in America than in most of the West (it is also high in West Germany and, in the form of suicide, high in Japan). But what about internal violence? Psychosomatic theory interprets coronaries and stomach ulcers as having a component of internal tension, violence which would be outwardly directed if the person could find a target. In theory, internal tension results from interrupted violence. It produces physical disturbance of the person's insides, and the process can be a killer. Rubin further reports that the United States and certain other economically advanced countries (England, Scandinavia, and most Anglo-Saxon countries) have high internal violence rates. In America, then, with our immense growth in GNP, we have the best of both worlds: high external and internal violence rates. The economic relevance is that the behavior necessary in an ambitious, aggressive people is also the behavior which triggers these manifestations of violence.

These facts support the profound doubt that the risk-taking behavior which seems required for economic growth is in all ways healthy; and they do illustrate Toffler's concept of future shock. As a clinical psychologist, I confess a concern for people under acute stress, including managers and others in high positions. I have seen them immobilized by apprehension for long periods of time, especially in corporate crises which require them to make some decisive action, when they hesitate, often unsure of the extent of their authority. These painful states are not to be denied.

**Some Limitations
of the Stress Concept**

In spite of the great weight of mental-health authorities,* there are a number of serious limitations in the stress theory

---

* We are tempted to stop and examine this problem of stress, as has been lucidly done in Levinson's book [39] or in German, by Jurg Peter Hausmann, in his authoritative summary of research in managerial stress.[40] It would prove a digression in that our main point is going to be that the dangers of managerial stress are real, but they are overstressed!

and some dangers of misapplication of the future-shock concept:

1. The remedy chosen by many managers who feel under pressure—the remedy being to seek change—is the very agent which, in Toffler's theory, causes the stress of future shock. How can the remedy for an ill be the ill itself?

2. The fact that so many people seek stress—and lots of it—thus disconfirms any simple notion that stress is noxious.

The first difficulty is the tendency of some managers to seek stress. If, as Toffler says, rapid change induces future shock, then a slowdown of change, a rest, would appear to be the ideal remedy for stress. But consider the typical response of many an executive who feels "up to here" or that he "has had it." He may do things like:

- play golf or ski
- go to Jamaica
- play poker
- watch a football game
- drive 6,000 miles to the coast and back

Now, some of these sound like a rest, and some do not. The common element is not that they are restful but that they all involve *change*. The vacationer, physically speaking, replaces one set of stresses (on the job) with another. If his problem is too much and too rapid change on the job, then how can it be that more change can be a good remedy?

The manager who wants a change usually does not go to bed, or at least not to sleep; he does not rest, although some old-fashioned physicians may still offer this as a general remedy. He does not return, bells slowly clanging, to the firehouse as in Selye's stress-recovery period. Fatigue is a very strange process. A teenager may come home "exhausted" from school, only to rush out eagerly to bowl or to ski; comes home again to collapse at dinner time; then brightens up and rushes out again to dance to midnight. If fatigue is thought to mean the exhaustion of a fixed supply of energy, none of this makes sense.

In brief, then, stress results from change, but the very curious remedy is more change rather than a reduction of it!

Another example of this paradox of stress: many managers instinctively resist retirement because they sense that being "put to pasture" will be an unhealthy life for them. I suspect that the death rates for persons just after they retire could establish that, for those of us who manage the retirement badly, it is indeed a death sentence. The paradox, of course, is that retirement, by *reducing* stress, becomes a danger to some.

Dys-stress versus Eu-stress

To remove this paradox, while admitting that stress has dangers, we will make a distinction which is fundamental to understanding this chapter, and even many other parts of this book:

- The noxious pressures of work, those that are dangerous and which, unwatched, can lead to serious illness and to emotional disturbance, will be called *dys*-stress.
- The other pressures of work, which are enjoyed because interesting, challenging, and even necessary to being a manager, will be called *eu*-stress.

To understand the first kind of stress, we read works like Levinson's and want the guidance of persons in the mental-health field. On the popular level, we may get some help from Ann Lander's columns or the local newspaper column on "watch your heart." But too much of this kind of reading is a bore. The reason is not that mental health is unimportant. Rather, it is that most of us would rather emphasize eu-stress ("eu" meaning happy, as in "euphoria"). There is a human *need* for pressure and for risk taking. If a manager does not find this in his job, he may create an uproar just to keep things interesting. Or he may just leave it.

EU-STRESS IN MANAGERS

The overpopularization of psychiatry, which no doubt is viewed with distaste by professionals as much as in this book, means that a variety of writers, columnists, and amateurs are applying psychiatric terms to situations for which they were not intended and which they confuse. There is a substantial need for more funds for mental-health facilities (in fact, in my home state of New Hampshire, it is a scandal how bad the need is); the campaigns for fund raising have contributed to the flow of overpopularized writing. The exaggerations and oversimplifications inevitable from such writing have become intolerable to some, like Thomas Szasz,[25] professor of Psychiatry at Syracuse Medical School, who maintains that much of our thinking about mental illness has created a *myth;* that creative behavior is often mistakenly called "sick"; that the very word sick, so very serviceable in talking about physical ailments, is often misapplied to human behavior in which no pain or danger to biological functioning is actually involved. It has even become fashionable in some urban groups to get a psychoanalysis whether one is sick or not.

While these popularizations and fashions are irritating and at times boring, they pose a real danger in leading to serious errors in the way we think about man. Samuel Klausner [19] was struck by the possibility that we have, during the last few decades of thought about human behavior, vastly overworked the passive and mechanical view of man:

> The assumption is that man, left to himself, would prefer not to strive. Individuals who in times of tranquility seek adventure, "look for trouble," "spoil for a fight," or go through life with "chips on their shoulders" are colloquially recognized as "deviant" types [p. v].

On the contrary, Klausner and his collaborators have collected evidence of many instances in which individuals "seek danger and search for problems resistant to solution, and even seek the stress, fear, or anxiety engendered by such encounters." Examples are:

■ mountain climbing, parachuting, and sporting competitions of all kinds
■ warfare and revolution
■ woman-mongering and various "infidelity games"
■ politics
■ starting a new business

Almost none of these examples makes rational sense. The risks are high (in politics, at least half the people lose), the costs are exorbitant, and the activity fatiguing. Much of the time, they do not even make moral sense, although the stress seekers do, at times, manage to find a moral justification. These moral justifications (e.g., college football builds character) are usually stale and unconvincing, and the woman-monger generally doesn't even bother to offer one.

The point is that men (and women) engage in activities which make no sense at all if we assume that people, left to their own devices, simply do not want trouble or striving; that they are basically tension reducers and stress avoiders; and that "health" means absence of pressure.

Jessie Bernard,[41] in a classic paper, coined the term "eu-stress," distinguishing it from dys-stress in the following ways:

■ Dys-stress is the kind of unpleasant state studied by Freud and Selye; eu-stress is pleasant, sought-out, and enjoyed stress.
■ Dys-stress is difficult and depressing, and the best thing we can say about it is that it builds character or is socially useful; eu-stress is exciting, "turns people on," and constitutes in Maslow's term, a "peak experience."
■ Dys-stress uses up human energy (the dys-stressed house-

wife gets worn out), and eu-stress *releases* it (she picks up at the party).

- Dys-stress often seems to go on and on, while eu-stress generally occurs in short bursts.

Economic Relevance of Eu-stress

Bernard suggests that the concept of *dys*-stress dates at least to the formulation of the Protestant ethic and to Puritanism in the United States. It is *the* way of life for people who assume responsibility and duty. They volunteer for disagreeable chores, and work on them consumes their energies. Thus the concept of stress was responsible, in part, for the rationale early capitalists gave for their activity. Perhaps it paid well, but they felt obliged to show what great personal sacrifices they were making. Work as "labor" was, indeed, the concept of classical economists. Until recent years they had no term for the work that managers do; it was a form of labor. Nor is there any clear way for financial analysts to place an economic value on a corporation's managers. They know that the value is there, but they do not know how to interpret it.

The labor that workers perform is often dys-stress to them and consumes energy; we "compensate" them for it. The labor that many managers perform is often eu-stress and releases energy; they do it just for the "hell of it." It has, in Herzberg's term,[42] "intrinsic" value to them. However, it would be absurd to leave money out of the picture; for many managers, it measures achievement and, to say the least, attracts their attention.

In general, eu-stress is the privilege of the affluent. Orientation to dys-stress is the effect of living a marginal existence. The hungry, sick, or insecure person has to conserve his energy against fatigue. Thus, the dys-stressed person does something different with his energy. He avoids pressure and demands, to save himself. This energy-conservation interpretation of stress suggests that countries in which food and survival are problems will not experience much stress seeking; Bernard points to the following examples of this association between stress seeking and affluence:

- Revolutions are led by prosperous people, not those suffering malnutrition (examples include the French Revolution and, more recently, the campus disorders).
- Hungry Chinese children, missionaries observed a few decades ago, did not play.
- During World War II, German occupation policies included imposing nutritional deficiencies on the population to discourage uprising.

As a result, the lower socioeconomic classes cannot enjoy tragedy on the stage; they can only listen to jokes or watch sadistic gags. The middle classes can only enjoy comedy. Only the affluent upper-middle and upper classes will deliberately court the stresses involved in suffering through a tragedy.

The Warrior Tradition in the Managerial Image

Business firms reflect a martial tradition in their language. The chief executive "wages war" on costs, and the company launches a "sales campaign." The manager is expected to be aggressive and put pressure on his competitors. The company has "strategy" in its expansion and "tactics" in its marketing.

This tradition dates to the idea of a warrior elite, although obviously this idea has been altered and distorted through its contact with the Protestant ethic and American cultural interpretations:

> The Warrior is essentially noble . . . frank and open in his exercise of the Will to Power. He has a strong body, good health, handsome features, noble bearing: he delights in the use of his strength in bodily combat, in the indulgence of all the fine

gifts of enjoyment his lusty senses afford him. He is capable, at his best, of flashing physical ecstasy.[43]

This is a very ancient, even a medieval, idea, but some of the tradition remains. Even though we refer to rational ideas like intelligence when outlining the qualifications of a manager, his aggressiveness is even more emphasized.[44] As in the ancient warrior image, managers are expected to look fit, keep in shape at the nearest athletic club, and maintain a combative frame of mind. Try to promote a brilliant but sickly looking, bearded, and poorly postured person as the new chief executive! The image won't fit, and the employees and stockholders will be shocked. He's not enough warrior.

The warrior image became modified in the nineteenth century into something called a "gentleman." The gentleman held the warrior's beliefs in his own nobility, his liking for combat, his assumption that he is beyond the bounds of the common morality, and his mistrust of the self-effacing. Rightly or not, the nineteenth-century gentleman-manager was considered by Veblen [45] to be exploitative and more recently by Fromm.[46]

The Rise of Bureaucracy and Professional Management

In the United States, the bureaucratic form of organization arose in reaction to the excesses of nineteenth-century politics and of the early industrial revolution. It was a moral idea. Managers *should* do things in a certain way, and other ways are taboo. Rules are written to ensure that they become more accountable. Professionalism (with its rationality, sense of responsibility, and its emphasis on science) further widened the gap from the nineteenth-century capitalist, until by 1930, it was possible to speak of a "managerial capitalism." [47]

Whatever the merits of professional management, it faces a residual skepticism among managers. This skepticism (toward the M.B.A., toward business schools, even toward corporate policy itself) expresses itself in persisting discomfort with the big organization, with the idea of business education, and in short, with those intellectual disciplines now said to be necessary to become a professional. For a time it seemed to me that the residual skepticism was of the older generation—the high school graduate who entered the business firm at an early age and, lacking a college degree, resented the newer generation who have it. I no longer think it quite that simple. We now have college-educated managers unconvinced by professionalism.

Instead, the problem seems to be the persistence of these very ancient life styles—the warrior and the gentleman—in managerial life. Excessive rationality and professionalism seem to many of us to deny the eu-stress-seeking impulses which are part of this life and give savor to it. In some big organizations the passionate risk taker is actively mistrusted while secretly admired.

In contrast, the professional manager is supposed to calculate everything. The image comes to mind of Robert McNamara with his cost effectiveness. (The old warriors in the Pentagon thought it *too* calculating.) But the new thought about military management has, in spite of them, filtered a long way. Bernard offers an example from the Air Force: "An Air Force training officer has been quoted as saying that he did not want heroes in his outfit; what he wanted was the well-trained technician who minimized risks and always took the lesser risk when he had the choice [p. 33]." [41] One could add that the Green Berets and commandos generally are mistrusted by "conventional-force" soldiers; such high-risk takers as the Berets are not quite "professional."

Leavitt and Whisler have even written a paper suggesting (how seriously I do not know) some replacement of middle managers by computers by the year 1980.[48] It is quite possible that the residual risk-taking or warrior tradition may well create resistances to the spread of computer technology. If so, this will not be merely because such middle managers fear for their jobs but more because something human goes out of management when its decision making becomes too scientific or too mechanical.

The Young Manager and the College Student

For several decades in American life it has not been fashionable to put up heroes and believe in them. Too many, perhaps, had been shown to have feet of clay, to be fallible, or to be stupid in their private lives. The happy warrior had so many failings. The image of corporate manager came to be one of a calculating professional, a cautious person without strong moral convictions who would not break step with his platoon.[15] Whether this image was fair or not, it has prevailed among the college students. At first, they responded with a growing but decisive lack of interest in corporate careers. They wanted jobs, many of them, which involved risk taking. They flocked into the Peace Corps, at $50 a month, until that went out of style.

Many college students have engaged in bitter denunciation of their college administrations on the grounds of lack of moral convictions.[49] Whether one agrees with their criticisms of the university or not, the change in the new student is unmistakable. Nor is it confined to the United States. We are observing a full-scale return of the romanticism of the nineteenth century, adapted of course to the new problems of the twenty-first. What this means for corporations who want to recruit college students for jobs is (1) trouble, and (2) opportunity. The trouble is obvious. The opportunity is not so obvious. It would seem that there is much opportunity for corporations to develop a new breed of younger managers if they can recognize and make use of this trend toward the go-for-broke life styles of earlier times. If the younger manager thinks of his corporation as a lockstep, bureaucratic, or excessively rational operation without opportunities for ideas, for risk taking, for eu-stress, he will either leave it or will deprive it of his best effort.

To some extent, this has always been a problem: how to give the young manager opportunities which do not demand experience he has not yet acquired. The point of the present analysis is that life styles among the young are going to make this problem more acute. The problem can be more readily solved if we recognize that what the young demand—opportunity to engage in go-for-broke styles of working as well as living—is the very eu-stress element which ought to be restored to managerial work generally. We cannot literally go back to the warrior, the gentleman, the nineteenth-century capitalist. These old forms of eu-stress seeking can be revived only if adapted to the modern corporate life.

The words used by the young in talking about their life styles are closer to eu-stress than we ordinarily recognize. The student wants to turn on; to find what Maslow calls a peak experience.[50] The eu-stress-oriented manager turns on in his work. This is the kind of work which the young want; they don't yet recognize corporation careers as providing it.

The Middle-aged Manager

Our main concern is, however, with the man who is manager now. This manager has inherited and, to some extent, may himself hold the dys-stress view of work. Work may be a *cost* to him, something that uses up energy, something that may even shorten his life and therefore is something for which he receives compensation. He is, in brief, tired. Bureaucracy is the organizational form for tired managers. The escape from this tedium need not be, as so many believe, a change of corporations. A change of definition of work is possible without a change of jobs. How this is done, by the corporation and by the individual, is to some extent the major problem of the fol-

lowing chapters. Here we are concerned more with the nature
of eu-stress. This is a subtle question. Perhaps its nature is
more fully understood if we consider a sample study of eu-
stress, Klausner's report on para-jumpers. After talking with a
number of them after a jump about the rise and fall of fear
(dys-stress) and enthusiasm or thrill (eu-stress) during the
jump, he reconstructed the typical jumping experience in the
following way:

■ Preparation for the jump: tension typically rises slowly
and is negative in feeling-tone (i.e., dys-stress); the jumper asks
himself, "Why did I ever get into a crazy thing like this? I'll
get killed!"

■ Preparation for the exit from the plane (stepping onto the
strut): tension slowly changes from negative to positive at the
point of the jump.

■ Just after the jump: the eu-stress quickly rises to a peak;
the jumper thinks, "Great! this is what I came for!"

■ Before the chute opens: apprehension, negative, "Will it
open? What if it doesn't?"

■ After it opens: exhilaration again.

■ Just before landing: apprehension, negative, "How hard
will I hit?"

■ Just after landing: great satisfaction. [p. 153–155] [19]

The point is simply that the same experience contains alter-
nations and mixtures of dys-stress and eu-stress. The tension
remains fairly high, but the *situation* changes. The dys-stress
or eu-stress depends on the specific situation at any point in
time. The point at which a jumper steps out on the strut (the
launching point) is, from an objective viewpoint, the most
dangerous part, yet fear starts dropping at that point, according to Klausner, because the jumper is *actively* engaging the
stress.

Is this not also true with the management of change and
conflict? A eu-stressed manager knows how to cope, has his

plans laid out. He does not passively suffer changes imposed from the outside or endure conflicts waged on him by others. The virtue of an active stance toward managing change and conflict is precisely this: it hurts less to make a hard tackle than to be run over by the ball carrier; it is less painful to initiate risk taking than to endure stress created by others. Hence we advocate that the manager *define himself* as a change seeker, a conflict manager. To do otherwise is to wait for trouble. Zorba the Greek put it well: "Life is trouble. Only death is not. To be alive is to . . . look for trouble." [51]

chapter six

Building a Eu-stress Organization

The chief executive is captive of his firm. In many ways, it seems that presidents have less freedom than the people working several echelons below them. Perhaps, on reading Chapter 5's suggestions for altering dys-stressed managerial styles into eu-stressed, such an executive would say, "Easy enough to do for the individual. I would have to change much more than the way I work at my own desk. I have a board, associates (who are the heads of related firms), regulatory agencies, subordinates, guidelines and policies, budgets, and customers. And my firm has traditions and old commitments." With all this in mind, he feels captive and may well wonder how he can change anything at all. This chapter is concerned with (1) how a firm characterized by a dys-stressed style of management got that way, and (2) what it can do to change that style.

SUGGESTED CHECKPOINTS

Managers can unwittingly create organizations which generate negative stress. Answering the following diagnostic questions will provide a rough idea of the extent to which a company's managers have put it into the negative frame of mind we call dys-stressed—full of problems and devoid of a positive future, an aging company too tired to fight or to innovate. At the same time, like all checklists, this one does no more than define the surface signs.

Presenting Goals

How clearly stated are the organization's goals? Who knows them: subordinates, associates, or superiors? Any firm's goals should be stated to everyone in the firm and in a measurable way—that is, in such a way that, at the end of the year, everyone can look at the facts and agree that "we made the goal," or "we did not." Such a goal is very much like a scientific hypothesis—it is something which can be put to the test of reality. Goal statements of this kind put pressure on people, but it is a refreshing kind of pressure. It releases them because it is the pressure of reality rather than that of a demanding boss.

How Clearly Are the Risks and Possible Gains Admitted? Part of the excitement of being a manager lies in the chance that he may realize outstanding achievement or experience calamitous failure. He can hit a homer or strike out. When a superior does not convey this excitement to his subordinates, he destroys a powerful incentive. He then must ask for cooperation on a voluntary basis, out of a sense of duty, out of personal liking, or even out of fear of job loss. Some company presidents hide their deepest troubles from almost everyone, feeling that they are paid to worry about the future and should not share their stresses with others. It is sometimes debated, "How much are the firm's employees entitled to know?" What is quite beyond debate, though, is that sharing risks and possible gains can help to communicate the excitement of managing.

Are Goals Stated in Terms of Environmental Opportunities? Goals can be stated for things which are entirely under a manager's control (some expenditures, for example) and also for things which are not (customer response to a new product, for example). It would seem unfair to hold a manager accountable for results which are not under his control. However, in a high-risk, eu-stress organization, *external* goals are the ones which count. An entrepreneur must be interested in the environmental response to his firm's products and operations; a bureaucrat, by contrast, is interested in his firm's *internal* processes, which are under greater control. Consider a business letter; how do we know that it is effective? (As the TV ad says—"Which do you want, good grammar or good taste?") The ultimate test of a business letter is whether it moves its reader—who is *not* under our direct control—to action, not whether the letter is written "properly" (which *is* under our control). Cost control is another good example. No one can deny the importance of cost control—it is usually faster to save money by reducing costs (which are under our direct control) than by increasing sales (which are not). But this logic cannot be pushed too far, for one can save even more money by shutting down the operation altogether!

Maintaining Unity

Is Unity Maintained by Goals—or by Policies? Every manager must have some kind of authority to make others act. He can choose between leading people by holding out to them a future goal toward which they move as a unity, and leading them because he is the duly constituted chief executive. The choice is somewhat like that between the leader in battle who leads troops toward an objective, and the peacetime leader who leads troops in a close-order drill. The battlefield-style manager judges everyone's performance, including his own, on the basis of whether they are progressing toward the goal. The drill-team manager judges according to whether each person is going through the motions properly. Hence, the first manager judges by results, the second by conduct.

During the Period When Goals Are Being Set, Are They Arrived at through Discussion or Simply Issued by a Manager as Directives? It would be pleasant to think that business firms could be democratic, but I am convinced such is not possible in the near future. The main point of this question, however, is not industrial democracy but the clarification discussion brings. If goals are not discussed with the people who must carry them out, they may be misunderstood; further, they may be blocked or hindered by others which were set earlier. A manager may be empowered to issue directives which set goals, but the subsequent power of those goals over the people who must carry them out, at least the power to release employees' energies, is dubious. A chief executive may well believe that he can push buttons at level 1 and generate flashing lights at level 5; that he can pound his desk and make the blotters jump up and down on his subordinates'. Dys-stress is transmitted this way but not eu-stress.

Fostering Relationships with the Outside

Are Results Judged against Outside Events or against Internal Standards? A manager can ask, "What results—out there in the market—did we get this year?" The results question can be phrased in terms of stock value (another kind of market), or public attitudes or respect for the firm, or union relations. All of these refer to results in the environment, results dependent on events over which the company has no direct control. A manager can, by contrast, ask, "Did you stick to your budget? Did you adhere to policy? Did you do what I asked you to do? Did you work hard?" These questions refer to internal operations under direct control and are oriented to those ways in which a person spends his company's time or other resources. They constitute a self-preoccupied system of evaluation. The system is essentially oriented to authority and has the greater possibilities for tyranny; it is consistent with a dys-stress system of management.

Are Ideas Brought in from Outside the Firm at a Sufficient Rate? The manager in a eu-stress system is likely to worry about excessively low turnover and promotion rates. In his view people should move around, move in and out. This movement generates activity and innovation. The bureaucratic-system manager worries rather about the costs of high turnover and prefers to promote not only within his organization but on a deliberate schedule, which does not disrupt people's careers and opportunities to learn their new jobs. It is better, he feels not to promote men "too fast for their own good." In brief:

System A (Eu-Stress Managers)	*System B (Bureaucratic Managers)*
1. Insist on clearly stated goals.	1. Control performance rather than goals.
2. Bring risks and gains into the open.	2. Conceal the stresses of their work.
3. Define goals in the environment.	3. Control the controllable.
4. Unify the group behind goals.	4. Unify the group behind policies.
5. Discuss goals before stating them.	5. Issue directives.
6. Judge performance against results in the environment.	6. Judge performance in terms of what the person has done or spent.
7. Emphasize ideas from the outside.	7. Emphasize "our thinking."
8. Believe in high turnover and rapid promotion.	8. Believe in low turnover and gradual opportunities for "our own people."

RECOVERING THE
ENTREPRENEURIAL SPARK

Much has been written in recent years about fostering more innovation and creativity in business firms. We will restrict ourselves here to discussing that particular kind of innovation which we call entrepreneurial. It differs from other innovations in several respects. First, it is not intended to solve the "suggestion box" kind of problem. Changes are wanted more with regard to market relations and the business firm's environments than to doing things better on the production floor or in the office. Second, entrepreneurial innovation cannot be generated by creating new organizational structures or new standards of work. In general, entrepreneurial thinking and behavior can be *released* but not caused, demanded, or created. The most an organization can do is to "get out of the way." However, this is not to say that simply increasing the freedom of individuals will result in a recovery of the entrepreneurial spark (bookkeepers, given their freedom, will merely engage in more bookkeeping). What seems to be most helpful is the freedom which comes from more environmental contact. But that is getting ahead of our story.

There are dozens of practical measures which could be taken to recover the entrepreneurial spark—and to use it productively. The risk of listing these measures is the inevitable tendency to substitute such a "laundry list" for actual understanding. The list will be presented, but the reader is cautioned to look for the concepts as he goes along. At the outset, the concept is essentially the nature of enterprise, as outlined in Chapter 1; the eu-stress style of management is the heart of that entrepreneurial way of operating, and the essence of eu-stress is the happy response to the pressure of goals, especially those which can be achieved in limited time spans.*

* This last point gives rise to one of the problems of eu-stress: that one can't sustain the very high note indefinitely; but a business firm must

The measures which can be taken to recover the entrepreneurial spark fall logically into several groups:

1. Incentives and motivation to work
2. Control systems regulating and coordinating work
3. Division of work among particular jobs and departments
4. Organization of work in relation to the future

Incentives and Motivations to Work

The nature of the motivation to work has been a matter of debate in recent years. We will not review this very interesting and fundamental debate (for example, Herzberg's position on the intrinsic quality of positive job satisfaction).[42] However, we do take the position that the evidence hardly warrants rejecting money as a necessary and fundamental incentive for managers. At the same time, the nature of managerial work is such that it can be—for the man properly chosen for his ability to tolerate stress—intrinsically or inherently rewarding. Recommended principles regarding motivation include the following.

1. *It is possible to release the motives of an entrepreneur, but it is not possible to create those motives if they do not exist.* No amount of frantic reorganization, such as has been done in large corporations in recent years, and also in such institutions as the church, can create entrepreneurial motives. This reorganization is not futile, but it must be planned in such a way that it releases those entrepreneurial motives which are present. Quite probably, every reorganization ought to be preceded by a census or survey to determine what kind of people (specifically, do they have the particular kind of "achievement needs" which we call entrepreneurial?) are there.

2. *The leadership appropriate to an enterprise is goal ori-*

nonetheless work toward long-term goals. Mobilization of maximum effort is possible only from time to time. Whoever wants to put the sailors on constant general quarters is eventually going to find them sleeping.

ented. Every leader sets goals, but not all leaders use the pulling power (their "let's go" quality, to use Marvin Bower's term [52]) of goals. Some leaders use the pushing power of the autocrat, and others the moral power of the bureaucrat. Evaluate the leadership for its style in this regard. If not enough key persons use pulling power, consider whether the way the company's organization, and the way policies are pushed on managers may be discouraging some natural leadership.

3. *The plans themselves should be used very fully by the leaders as the primary way of ensuring that goals have the fullest possible room for exerting their enormous pulling power.* We have all seen plans which were expensively designed, elegantly written, and shelved. They never really became the chief executive's plan. Or else he became timid in the face of doubts from his managers about the plans. The chief executive may feel very intensely that a goal is important, but it is the plan which provides the chance for momentum to build up around that goal. I recall a management-training program through which we ran over 600 middle managers and soon-to-become top managers. Its second week was devoted to long-range planning as a prime managerial tool. We stressed that it was the chief executive's tool, and that their role was to help him use it. The question inevitably arose: "What do we do if he doesn't want to formulate and follow a long-range plan?" The answer is nothing at all. Or else, scheme to get rid of the chief executive and bring in a professional.

4. *Money should be distributed in an entrepreneurial way, to the fullest extent possible.* We are speaking of salary, bonus, and other such money to individuals. I carefully avoid saying compensation. Compensation is a bureaucratic term, meaning to compensate to the individual the toil he has contributed, or compensate him for the position he holds.

Entrepreneurial pay is primarily an incentive for future results. The incentive is credible, of course, only if it has some relation to the results achieved this year. But basically, the company *invests* in entrepreneurial managers. This may mean paying some people more than they are worth, if it appears that such pay will bring in superior results. Such payments arouse the interest of managers and give them a yardstick for measuring what the company thinks their *potential* is. Thus, money has both an attention-getting and a self-measuring function, as Patton [53] reminds us. This is not to say that its compensation function is irrelevant. There should be some compensation for risk, for example. Furthermore, the company's manager of salary administration has to contend with the very keen sense of justice people have on the subject of money —a salary completely out of balance with the external market (what are they paying industrial engineers now?) and out of balance with the internal market (the prestige structure of jobs within the corporation) will cause tensions.* Finally, it does seem wise to compensate people for aging itself—i.e., for honoring the universal demand for seniority prerogatives. This demand is present among managers as well as union members. But these bureaucratic features in managerial pay structure should be the minor features, sufficiently present to prevent undue tension and injustice, but not so dominant that the admittedly materialistic excitement of money is lost.

Coordination of Work

A manager's chief function is to allocate resources. More precisely: the entrepreneurial manager's chief function is to muster, allocate, and focus resources upon environmental goals in such a way as to increase those resources. Some people read this last phrase "make a profit." But it refers not only to an economic margin but also to the increase in resources of talent, knowledge, and market position. Think of the manager as

---

* Homans's [54] balance theory helps us understand the sense of justice involved in compensation.

a lad with a magnifying glass. He holds the lens in such a way as to focus the sun's rays (the resources) upon a piece of dry wood (the environmental opportunity). Some would say he brings together two energy sources (sun and wood). Still better, he releases energy. Now we are concerned with the particular way in which entrepreneurs release energy from organizations—how do they hold the lens?

5. *The entrepreneur enlarges resources by the way he uses them; and as a generalist, he is interested in all kinds of resources, not one or two pet types.* It is not difficult to spot the kind of manager who is hoarding resources and whose primary policy is to use as little as possible. The point to check is whether corporate policies and practices have encouraged this hoarding behavior. Consider costs: in the short run there is no doubt that money is a fixed resource, so that the less we spend the more we have. In the long run the same policy becomes unreasonable. I remember a long debate over whether to close a certain plant which had been losing money for years. It was situated in an area where there was excess production capacity among the competitors. The younger managers were eager to close the plant; the older ones, strangely reluctant. How could this plant continue to operate, at a loss, year after year; it did not make sense. Finally, one of the old hands pointed out that while this particular plant should probably be closed, there were many places in the firm at which the same argument— save by closing down the plant—could be used; in fact, in sufficiently lean times, one could even propose closing down the entire corporation and "save" it all. This paradox results from mixing up two different time spans: short- and long-run wisdom.

Managers, in my observation, tend to have particular resources which are their favorites to tend to. Some develop more market contacts; others are more financially oriented. This specialization is not entrepreneurial. Entrepreneurs are generalists interested in all resources. There are the "M's"—

money, men, markets, and manufacturing facilities. There is also knowledge, and there is time. All of these resources can be expanded except time. Any of them can be easily neglected by the manager who is riding another "hobby horse," and this is a cardinal sin. The entrepreneurial manager does not play such favorites—not if he seriously wants to build an *organization,* which is just a word for the focusing lens which combines these different resources into a single powerful thrust toward the future. How do we translate the concepts of resources management into a recommendation for action? Perhaps the simplest action is to take an inventory of all resources periodically; ask how recently and how fully each of them has been used; and whether this use has been such as to expand the value of that resource.

6. *Make serious use of the task-force form of organization.* The task force is ordinarily a group of managers and specialists drawn from more than one department or division, chosen for ad hoc purposes, or relevance to a particular goal ("project"). The task force is of limited tenure and is headed by a leader who leads by goal rather than by personal or bureaucratic authority. Most firms, I would guess, cannot replace the bureaucratic and hierarchic forms of organization with task forces. They have to cultivate the art of setting up and using task forces without undue disturbance to, or strain of, the routine arrangements. The importance of the task force in the present context is that it identifies and breeds entrepreneurs. The McCormick Company's "multiple-management" (or "junior board") system provided just such an opportunity to identify promising younger managers and give them a chance to show what they could do in useful assignments outside their regular jobs. However, the task force is not only a management-development device. Occasional service on a properly chosen task force, backed fully by top management and undertaking work on significant goals, can invigorate managers of any age.

7. *All managers should be able to measure some significant part of their work against results in the environment.* This is a way of saying everyone should ideally "interface" with some part of the environment (see no. 9). Unfortunately, this is not the way corporations have been built. The typical organization structure does not bring every manager in contact with the external reality which keeps the corporation in business or determines its prosperity: customers, investors, suppliers, regulatory agencies, unions, potential new customers, competitors, and segments of the "knowledge industry." (This last industry refers to the producers and marketers of scientific and technical information, the media, and the educational industry. Corporations without substantial contact these days with the knowledge industry will suffer in a variety of ways; it is a prime resource.) Instead of showing every manager in contact with one or more of these exteriors, the typical organization chart shows the manager primarily in contact with those above and below him in the hierarchy, and perhaps in communication laterally, but all within the corporation. Some charts even imply that the only environment interfacing with the company is the customers directly served by the salesmen, who are as likely as not placed on the lowest or first echelon. As echelons rise above the lowly contact man, they move away from the marketplace until the president seems to sit in distant grandeur on his throne. We grant that the managers know this is not completely so; but we are afraid that the chart is telling at least a partial truth. There are various ways to ensure that managers measure some significant part of their work against results in the environment. A simple example would be to require that some goals be set in each manager's plan for the coming year which can be met only by action in the environment and with results measurable only by the response of some person or feature of the environment.

8. *Managers should make more use of "PERT charting" than they do.* This is not the place for a technical explanation

of **PERT** charts ("Program Evaluation in Real Time," as I would prefer to call it), which is available in other places (see especially Roman [55]). The concept is the important thing. The essential concept in realtime charting is the simultaneous representation of goals and their interrelationship. Most of us can set clear-cut goals, one at a time. Many of us go on to make lists of the different goals to which we are committed; and it is not unusual to place them all on a common time line, to see what is coming due when. What is ordinarily missing in these linear- or simple-planning devices is the *network*. If one's job is a coherent whole, there should be such a network of interrelationships among separate goals. In fact, if one cannot find such interrelationships (achievement of one goal helping in the achievement of subsequent goals), there is a good question of whether it is a coherent job. When there are these networks in a job, it is possible to build resources, as was demanded earlier (see no. 5)—the entrepreneur increasing his resources by the way he uses them. Thus, when one achieves goal A first, goal B becomes easier; whereas goal B would perform no service—provide no resource—for A. Example: it may be logically possible to research a new market and train salesmen for that market at the same time, but doing the research first may provide more creative ideas about how to train the salesmen.

The Division of Work

The modern corporate structure is fractured into specialties whose vision is less than entrepreneurial. This is not only due to the era when corporate structures were generally devised (when the doctrines were autocratic and bureaucratic). It also reflects the powerful influence of the knowledge industry itself, which continually fractionates as it grows. We have, for example, many different kinds of medical personnel now—for the simple reason that there is more medical knowledge than there was. This may be unfortunate, but it is probably historically inevitable. Finally, fractionation reflects the effects of size itself. As first-echelon people increase, eventually they need more than one boss; as the second-line bosses increase in number, they eventually need a third-line boss. These bosses are new specialists. Further, beyond a certain size (usually the breaking point is 100), the group needs a full-time personnel administrator. At other breaking points, still other specialists appear. And as the specialties themselves increase in diversity and number, somebody has to coordinate *them.*

This account of the effects of growth in size is not news to the reader; the real point is that specialists tend to lose contact with the environment. The analogy might be made to the growth of a circle. As the radius increases, its area will increase faster than its circumference—the part which touches the circle's "environment." The new specialties which appear as the organization increases are part of its area—they are made necessary by the size of the organization itself and tend to service the organization, not the environment. We do grant that there are also environmental specialists—labor-relations men, financial men, etc.—who study selected parts of the environment. But it is quite possible to be interested in the environment and not be entrepreneurial (opportunity seeking) in that interest. At any rate, as the corporation grows in size, it ordinarily knows less and less in an entrepreneurial way about the environment, in our view. Can anything be done about it? Here are some suggestions.

9. *Increase the interfaces with the environment.* One learns to think like an entrepreneur primarily by acting like one—by surveying an environment and finding opportunities in it. This can mean markets, customers, or other environments. The notion that only salesmen and marketing specialists are entitled to search for opportunities is an exceedingly dangerous point of view. To give managers more opportunity for such interaction one may rotate them through departments which interface with the environment: sales, merchandising, advertising, law, labor relations, public relations, personnel re-

cruiting, even lobbying (perhaps a tour of duty with the trade association of which the firm is a member). IBM once broke up its selling pattern by creating new teams: instead of a salesman calling on prospects, a team of salesman and engineer did the calling.

Managers can interface with the outside world by reading (other than house organs!), taking courses at a university, attending executive-development programs. Their wives can insist on a social life which is not too heavily inbred with the company's. One corporation president got his executives to agree that they would not play cards with each other. The intent was to avoid gambling debts (and ill feeling); the effect was also to reduce the inbred quality of the company's social life. This same corporation president also instituted another practice (no more popular than the first): each executive was required to join one of the company's sales drivers on his route, one day a month. He donned a sales driver's uniform, drove to the pickup point early in the morning, rode the truck with the driver all day. The effect was to prevent the kind of snobbery which sometimes invades the executive suite. It could not have hurt the labor relations in that company either.

10. *The entrepreneurial work load should be as high as possible.* I once heard an oil company's executive vice-president remark that the best way to maintain morale is to keep the work force small enough to keep busy. The first reaction to this remark might be that this was a nineteenth-century exploiter of labor speaking. Not so in this man's case! In fact, I have heard a union business agent make the same remark off the record about a production department—that many of its grievances and tensions were due to overstaffing. But the high work-load policy does not make quite clear that some kinds of high work load can be destructive. It is—for managers—the *entrepreneurial* work load (not the bureaucratic load nor the

autocratic pressure) which ought to be high. How can we tell the difference?

One way is to tackle the job description of every manager with this problem in mind, and revise it along the following lines:

- Arrange the duties in order of priority.
- Prune the lowest-ranked duties (as many as possible).
- Add to the top of the list (to the high priority end) only new duties which are entrepreneurial in character.

The job has been properly revised if (*a*) it has increased its interfaces with the environment; (*b*) it has reduced paperwork and similar routines; and (*c*) it turns on or provides more incentive to the job holder. In general, such a job would now appear of more intrinsic worth in Herzberg's system.[42] When this has been done with a variety of managers, some jobs will be found which stubbornly resist this kind of reorganization and revitalization. Those are the jobs where overstaffing is more likely to exist, and perhaps many of them can be eliminated altogether. True, some managers may resist this process. Every job acquires what might be called "barnacles"—time-consuming routines which appear useful work but which have lost much of their original justification. The manager acquires some affection for these routines. But the ship ought to be put in the yard for barnacle removal; every manager should remove them himself. It is not only his right to do so, but also his obligation, since barnacles on the job ordinarily generate bureaucratic work for other managers. Perhaps report writing and paper accumulation are the easiest examples of how one bureaucrat creates routine pressures on others.

Developing a Future-oriented Organization

Alvin Toffler has a number of constructive suggestions in his book, *Future Shock,*[17] for learning to live with the frightening pace of change in society. We need similar suggestions for developing managers who can take change and who can manage it. Managing change is the chief task of the entrepreneurial manager, as we outlined in Chapter 2. This problem has several layers. It is like peeling off layers of the onion. We begin by noting the outer layer, peeling off the definition of the new entrepreneur as a manager of change or change seeker. But then we find under this another layer: the manager who must be prepared for risk taking and especially for conflict, the inevitable consequence of all significant change. And yet another layer of the onion now appears to view: the manager who must live with the personal stress which goes with or follows risk taking and conflict.

11. *Innovation is the chief function of the entrepreneurial manager, and there should be as great a proportion of such managers as the kind of industry can assimilate.* The significance of innovation has been too well spelled out in Drucker's writing to warrant repetition here. We might add, however, that there is also a place for the bureaucratic manager, and the proper portion will vary with the department and type of industry. For his airline tickets, the traveler wants crisp, bureaucratic efficiency; iron control in the cockpit of the plane; precision in the operation of the train, the electricity, and the delivery of milk in the morning. Even so, while we used to think of utilities as a good place for bureaucrats, the massive new ecological problems now being handed to airlines, power industry, and public health demand innovation. The proportion of entrepreneurs in these fields should increase. I, for one, would like more enterprise in inventing new baggage-handling systems and less risk taking in the production of big new planes. (But that is merely one passenger's ignorant point of view.) Perhaps transportation illustrates as well as any industry the partnership of enterprise and bureaucracy; to recover the efficiency of commuter trains, we shall have to innovate. Once again, while it has been useful to contrast enterprise

with bureaucracy through this book, it is more *realistic* to stress their interdependence. The general view here, however, is that almost any industry needs a greater proportion of entrepreneurs than it has.

12. *Managers should be selected for, and trained for, combat.* What is worth fighting for is innovation which looks productive. There is no guarantee that combative managers will not fight for other reasons—engage in petty office politics, for example. But it is assumed that those who shrink from conflict (because they are poor at it) will also shrink from innovation. One important limitation on this recommendation: it is intended only for corporations organized along entrepreneurial lines. In autocratic corporations (those dominated by one-way power relationships and which are exploitative rather than opportunity seeking), it is foolish and perhaps dangerous to select and train managers for conflict.

13. *Managers should be selected and trained for greater stress tolerance.* The ability to "take it" is a prime requirement for the entrepreneurial role. Still better is the ability to take it and like it. The eu-stress style is that of the happy warrior, not the reluctant sufferer from pressure. In general, the development of stress-tolerant managers is like competitive sports: gradually exposing the individual to tougher and tougher situations. There is no warrant for sudden pressures for which individuals are not emotionally prepared; they should not be greatly put out of their depth. But in general, young managers can probably take more than older managers assume; eu-stress is in many respects a young man's life style.

14. *Managers should be selected and trained for a hopeful view of the future.* It is not difficult to determine who is future oriented. Ask a manager why he is doing what he is doing at the moment; he will explain the result which he expects. Then ask when he will know that result; the time span between present action and future result gives a rough measure of the depth of his "future vision." Managers with pessi-

mistic views of the future will ordinarily confine themselves to very limited time spans, and they feel much more comfortable entirely in the present. A similar test may be applied to the manager's plans. The plan will have a certain depth of future vision. It will also take account of social changes. Note whether the social changes foreseen in that plan resemble those foreseen by the more sophisticated futurologists.[56] Note also whether the manager is primarily interpreting those social changes as merely negative "problems," or whether he is searching his understanding of them to find positive features, or ways in which they may be turned into opportunities. This is known as making virtue out of necessity. It is not, however, the same as being a Pollyanna. We should distinguish between the manager who is an incurable optimist and one who is constantly hopeful. The first manager has a pleasant vision of the future because he ignores the potential disasters and unpleasant facts in it (he's a tough client for the insurance man). The second manager—the hopeful one—has a very different vision of the future. His is the future which takes account of the facts and tries to use them in a positive way.

One can train managers in hopeful perspectives by working with them on their plans. I have found it desirable to work with them as a consultant on their personal plans—their "scenarios"—as well as on their plans for work. These are, in the creative manager, closely intertwined. By asking them hard questions (if they are ignoring potential disasters and negative possibilities) or creative questions (if they are too fearful), one can coax many a bureaucrat into being a risk taker.

LIFE CYCLE OF THE FIRM

John Gardner once wrote:

> Like people and plants, organizations have a life cycle. They
> have a green and supple youth, a time of flourishing strength,

and a gnarled old age. . . . But organizations differ from people and plants in that their cycle isn't even approximately predictable. An organization may go from youth to old age in two or three decades, or it may last for centuries. More important, it may go through a period of stagnation and then revive. In short, decline is not inevitable.[57]

What is quite clear is that a business firm is exceedingly difficult to revive, renew, reinvigorate. Some try reorganizing. Do the somewhat frantic restructurings which frequently occur among today's large corporations really revitalize those firms? These reorganizations seem more like minor automobile restylings—fenders are reshaped, dashboards widened, wider color choices made available, all without fundamentally improving the safety, comfort, serviceability, or reparability of the car.

The primary reason for this inertia is that a firm is not purely and simply a rational machine. It is what anthropologists would call a *culture.* It has a common internal lingo, customs, value systems, and a common history. These features provide stability and strength. It is likewise a source of inertia; cultures change very slowly. Perhaps John Gardner learned that the Health, Education, and Welfare Department was more like a culture than a plant. One feature in particular which corporate firms share with culture is a history. The importance of a corporate history is this: in the very process of becoming a business firm, an organization undergoes experiences which it comes to regard as the source of fixed truths. During that history, a firm has met certain problems and responded to them; as it responds successfully, it begins to *believe in the way in which it solved each problem:* the problem-solving technique thereby becomes a fixed habit. (Companies have habits, just as individuals do.)

The bureaucracy in the firm regards those fixed habits as the primary source of policy. They continue to enforce the policy, regardless of whether it gets results in the environment. The bureaucracy is blind to those results, not because it is dull-witted, but because it does not interface with or interact with the environment. As time passes, and the firm grows from very small to large and to very large, two forces produce an increase in the power of the bureaucracy. One of them is the inertial force of custom, due to the culture-like characteristics of the firm. The other force is structural, due to the effects of size. In general, with increases in size, there are changes and usually reductions in the interfacing with the environment.

Most of the recommendations above (no. 1 through no. 14) are designed to overcome these inertial and structural blockages of the entrepreneurial impulse. Others among these recommendations are designed to locate, and perhaps encourage or even develop, great managers. As to whether great managers are born or made, who knows? Once I studied the case histories of 180 managers.[58] Some had national eminence; some had high reputations within their own industries, but were not nationally known; and some were regarded only locally as successful and effective. The research questions were: What kind of behavior do observers attribute to these managers? What kind of work methods do they themselves describe? In particular, how do these kinds of behavior differ between managers who are eminent and those who are effective but not eminent?

Two differences appeared:

■ The eminent managers showed greater variability in human relationships, while the local men were aggressive or autocratic.

■ The eminent managers were oriented more toward very long-term results, some working toward goals many years in the future; the local men were oriented to shorter-term goals.

The second finding is particularly relevant here: what is the meaning of the long-term perspective? I would suggest that eminent managers—very entrepreneurial types of men, I might add—derive considerably more energy from their goals than other people do. They pursue some dreams, aspirations, hopes, and blueprints for new enterprises which, to most people, would seem idle, impractical, or unlikely because so far in the future. This is the nature of genius, however; it pursues improbable possibilities but in such a perceptive way as to realize them.

Such an interpretation of the entrepreneur explains why he has a greater interest in the environment than other people have. Once committed to long-term goals, he will find himself in disastrous positions unless he pays very close attention to social trends and economic possibilities. He is an ecologist; to be otherwise would be to lose his shirt.

chapter seven

Training Directors: Experts, Professionals, or Entrepreneurs?

Training directors rarely become corporation presidents. The answer to "Why not?" is not only of interest to them but has a bearing on why *experts* have trouble becoming anything other than experts. Granted, experts have an interesting and useful specialty and may be better paid than many a generalist, with a lot more security than the entrepreneur. But experts in any field ought to know some of the factors which keep them in that role, in case they should want to leave it.

Let's begin by avoiding circular answers—such as, the experience training men get does not qualify them for general management posts. In the first place, it may not really be true in all cases, and in the second case this kind of explanation doesn't really explain anything at all. It is a circular answer and therefore a stupid remark to say "training men are not qualified because they're not qualified."

How about prejudice? The training man, like other specialized experts, is bypassed when he ought to get consideration,
just because people have silly prejudices about training. We
can enlarge on this answer. First, we can argue that line managers have prejudices against many staff services—but why?
Second, line managers have a silly prejudice toward lines of
work which deal in intangibles or "software." A third prejudice is against departments in the corporation which use up
the budget rather than *contributing* income. This prejudice
looks upon training as one of the luxuries which can be safely
cut back in hard times, or as an operation which is not really
a fundamental part of the business anyway.

The trouble with prejudice as an explanation, even if we
believe it to be true, is that it does not tell us what to do
about it. We dismiss the inappropriate experience and prejudice explanations as either silly, false, or useless. Instead it is
suggested that:

- The training manager can win a reputation for being a
tough-minded thinker by engaging in tougher-minded evaluation of his programs.
- The training manager can become a general manager by
managing the training department.
- The training manager can become an entrepreneur because all entrepreneurs are in the "people business"—those
who design and conduct training are clearly in the business of
understanding human motivation.

To move in some new directions, the training manager is
going to have to avoid some unprofitable old directions. The
training manager comes from a history of entrapment in some
narrow views of the business enterprise and of his own contri-
butions to it. In this chapter I hope to make clear that the history of the training field has left in him some very bad habits
which should be discarded. At the same time, it has offered
him some remarkable opportunities which he should seize.

A SHORT HISTORY OF TRAINING

Training is ordinarily defined as one of the staff services provided by the personnel department. It therefore suffers from the semantics of being called "staff" and "personnel." It can escape those problems—and those prejudices—only if it is fairly clear on the accidents of history which gave it the problems.

The Pecking Order
among Business Functions

The terms "line" and "staff" are being criticized in industrial thought today as being largely without meaning. However, they have a very old history, and words die slowly. Where did they come from?

Staff is a military term dating back to the military recognition that front-line troops need to be backed up by some specialties. First, there were logistics and engineering, and later many other staff services were added. There are as many such staff services as there are technologies. Nowadays there is a very heavy ratio of staff (or support) services to front-line (or fighting) troops. For every rifleman or "grunt" there are several support people like tractor drivers, switchboard operators, mail carriers, radio operators, etc. These support positions carry the implication that they are not essential. The riflemen look down on—even as they envy—these rear-echelon people.

In industry, some of the terminology unfortunately was carried over. The production department was the first line department. Eventually, the sales department came into its own. In some companies, it *is* the line, and the *production* department is one of its support services. In general, however, the attitude by both sales and production is that they are the line departments. They say to other departments, sometimes in a joking way but more often with some feeling, "We pay your bills. We make the money. You fellows think up new ways to

spend it and raise the overhead." A company can create flak—
adverse comment—if it promotes other than a line manager
(someone who came up through production or sales) to top
posts, and the title, "general manager" is ordinarily used to
refer to a production or marketing unit or a combination.

In brief, then, to label something staff or support is to
imply that, to a degree, it is not quite at the heart of the business, not quite entrepreneurial.

The Pecking Order
among Staff Functions

Suppose someone outside the sales or production departments is so superior a candidate that the board of directors
cannot pass him by. Even among these other departments—
the so-called staff departments—there is still a hierarchy of
consideration. It would run something like this:

Pecking Order of Staff Services

1. Financial V.P. (most acceptable)
2. General Counsel
3. V.P., Business Acquisition
4. V.P., Advertising
5. V.P., Personnel (least acceptable)

If there is a Vice President, R&D, he might well come ahead
of Personnel. The training director, who probably reports to
the Vice President, Personnel, is not in line for a good shot at
the top. Not fair! you say. But this isn't to say that the pecking order makes sense, or needs to be this way, but that it
probably is that way. Why? I would guess—to the extent that
there is this hierarchy—that it reflects the age of the staff function. The older the staff function the better integrated it is
into the firm's traditions. Test this out: we had financial departments long before personnel. And even the priority given
to the production and sales departments might be explained

on this basis. Thus the personnel (and even more the training) functions are among the more recent.

The trouble with this explanation—although there may be some truth in it—is it doesn't tell us much what to do. Just letting time pass is not going to help training men gain. They are still among the younger staff functions. Also: the explanation does not explain why newer functions (like R&D) move ahead so very quickly.

The Canard That Experts Take Fewer Risks

Persons in jobs traditionally considered line often allege that the experts occupy safer jobs, like the rear-echelon support people in battle. The rifleman believes he lives a harder life as well as a shorter one. When he makes a bad decision—in production or sales—the whole company knows it. That is, he sticks his neck out more, and is more likely to get it chopped off. But his main point is that every decision he makes is more vital; he believes, deep down, that it is usually his work which wins or loses the battle.

Whether experts take fewer risks or not, the belief that they do leads to occasional mumbling (particularly in bad times) that the company could "clean out the bureaucracy" and not really suffer much. General managers know this is false, but at times they do not make it clear what they do believe about the value and relevance of staff work.

Part of the reason expert decisions are not regarded as vital is that they cannot fully be explained to amateurs. The high-level transactions regarding stock splits are understood by perhaps 1 percent of the employees of a company. Such decisions are technical decisions. The technologist cannot hope to be understood by everyone and should not be surprised if people take little interest in what they do not understand. On the other hand, everyone understands (or thinks he does) the production process because the product is concrete and tangible:

there it is, all wrapped up and ready to deliver. As for selling, everybody knows what a sale is! But not everybody, unfortunately, understands the role of the credit and collections department in translating the sales into dollar income. Thus the collections manager lacks the prestige, in some companies, he would have if his work were more clearly understood. But the mistakes he makes are perhaps less visible; the trade-off is, he takes less risk.

The Allegiance of the Expert

Experts often have ties to organized groups outside the corporation. They do this because their qualifications are very often determined by specialized knowledge shared with persons in other corporations. Where the general manager attains his knowledge of the corporation by long service within it, the staff manager gains much of his knowledge through specialized study and experience outside the corporation. The general counsel, for example, is part of the legal profession. And there are: a Purchasing Officers Association, a Training Directors Association, Operations Research groups, and so on, all representing ties outside the corporation.

These ties may not be very strong, but they do imply that a staff manager has expertise not unique to his particular company or industry. Implicit in this expertise is the implication that he may not quite be as much an "organization man" as those who lack such ties.

Eminence in these outside associations often does not help the specialist very much within his organization. One example I recall: one year an engineer was elected the outstanding (in the United States) manager of his specialty by his national engineering association; the very next year he was fired by his corporation. He was fired for reasons peripheral to the main function of his job, but the important point is that the corporation's particular reasons far outweighed his national eminence. As I recall the case, even before the firing, the engineer was somewhat disillusioned that so few in the company had much interest in his award.

The logical reason for many staff associations is their common technical base. Lawyers share a body of knowledge. Plant physicians are still medical men. Comptrollers share a common knowledge of data-processing and accounting disciplines.

We may be approaching a time when nothing will be defined as a staff service if it lacks a fairly elaborate technical base. Whether or not this comes to pass, however, the technology of a staff service will probably remain one of the more important reasons for its position in the pecking order of staff services. But it is problematic in the following sense. Technology is an occasion for both jealousy, on the part of line managers because they do not understand, and respect, once those managers concede that the technology provides a real payoff for the firm's operations. Legal personnel rose closer to the top of the hierarchy in part because they knew something no one else knew; at the same time, they occasionally suffered from the traditional American impatience with and suspicion of the law.

From this discussion we can summarize five factors which determine the status of a staff service and ultimately may limit even the eligibility of an outstanding manager of that service for a higher post in his company:

- The term "staff service" itself implies a nonvital function.
- Integration into the firm depends partly on the age of the staff service.
- Staff decisions appear to be less risky.
- Staff services have external allegiances.
- Staff services have a technical base.

The Personnel Bureaucracy

Training faces an additional problem not suffered by all staff services. It is ungracious to say it out loud, but its assignment to the personnel area of staff services places it within a department which is sometimes the most bureaucratic of all. This statement is unfair to many aggressive and professional personnel departments, and therefore a more specific yardstick is offered by which the particular department can be evaluated, to decide how bureaucratic it is. The following characteristics refer to "bureaucracy" as defined in this book; a department is relatively more bureaucratic if it:

- is a rules-making or rules-enforcing body
- invests a considerable portion of its budget in manual writing and record keeping
- measures its work in terms of what it does within the company rather than against what it accomplishes in the company's environment
- views expenditures as costs rather than as investments
- plans only passively (i.e., following the leads of other departments rather than itself seeking to improve the corporate operations)

Training managers, to the extent they work within personnel departments, take on some of the traditional viewpoints of those departments. That is, the training chief may bureaucratize the training function itself. To illustrate, consider the left-hand column of the attached figure (Figure 7.1).

Neither training nor personnel departments need to be totally bureaucratic. This may be their historic role, but can they not escape it? Some have. But some of the very practical difficulties faced by training men, which have grown out of their history, should be understood.

The Rapid Change
in the Training Department

The training function in United States industry probably came into its own during World War II. In defense industries, labor migration, manpower turnover, and shortages of skills

Bureaucratic model	Entrepreneurial model
1. The training department administers programs (i.e., production routines) which can be designed once and for all, run, and periodically checked for conformity to plan and efficiency in costs.	1. The training department manages programs (i.e., plans of action) which must be constantly redesigned and checked for their integration within the company and for their subsequent results.
2. Objectives of the program are behavioral: to get the trainee to do his work in a standardized way.	2. Objectives of the program are goal-oriented: to get the trainee to work in a way which will have an impact on his environment.
3. Since standardized methods can be used to obtain standardization in behavior, it is possible to purchase programs "off the shelf."	3. Every program must be adapted to the particular environment in which the trainees are going to perform, even if, in some respects, it is purchased off the shelf.
4. Effectiveness of a program can be determined during the program, especially by asking whether it was done according to plan.	4. Effectiveness of a program for a particular company cannot be determined until after it has been tried and the trainees' subsequent work checked.
5. Almost all expenditures are for operating the program. (Few are for design or evaluation.)	5. A sizable share of the expenditures are for design (choosing the results wanted and working these back into design) and evaluation (checking results).
6. Cost control is exercised by keeping them within normal limits for such training.	6. Cost control is exercised by keeping them proportionate to their results.

Figure 7.1

compelled companies to upgrade the status of and the investment in their training departments. Here was a case in which the status of a staff service outran its technology—there was not much research-based knowledge for training managers to apply in solving their problems. For example, an extraordinarily simpleminded method, called "training within industry" (TWI) was devised and circulated as a basic program to follow in designing training. Examination of TWI shows it to be a series of logical steps, easily explainable to a foreman, hard to question—TWI was common sense. Its essential idea could be put on a wallet-sized card and carried around the factory. It had no technical basis at all. That is, it did not rest on any research knowledge of how human skills get changed.

This commonsense era of training was replaced, following the war, by a rapidly growing technology; in rapid succession, new knowledge and/or hardware bases for training were developed and applied. Examples of the new technology were:

- software designs from the behavioral sciences, giving rise to training methods such as role playing and sensitivity training
  - programmed instruction and teaching machines
  - simulation
  - computer-aided instruction
  - video tape playback

In the late 1940s the training manager began receiving tasks at successively higher levels in the corporation, i.e., where he might earlier have begun with devising training programs for production workers, he moved up to training supervisors, and eventually participated in developing managers.

The most significant postwar movement in training was management development. Companies experienced initial difficulties in asking lower-echelon training managers to enter this field; how, after all, could training personnel provide instructive experiences for managers and executives higher in the pecking order than themselves? By 1970, however, the American Society of Training Directors was able to retitle itself *Training and Development* and could honestly contend that, of all the staff services, it was *the* one which was most significantly responsible, in the sense of program design, for developing managers.

The training manager was, nevertheless, in a state of confusion. No generally recognized qualifications for his post were set. He was, and still is, as likely to come from a line department, without particular educational and experiential qualifications, as to be specifically trained for his job. To design meetings for training directors, under these conditions, requires the creativity of a Leonard Nadler and other such program planners.

Into this confusion came all the new training technology. The training director greeted the rise of training technology with a mixture of attitudes: ambivalence, to put it mildly. For example, who is not intrigued by the instant insights provided by watching one's performance on the video tape replay? On the other hand, the technical skills required to design and operate video tape-based training are numerous, and few possess them. A more frightening example is programmed instruction. The technical complexity of teaching machines or their offshoot-designs appears quite great to someone not acquainted with the conditioning technology used in the psychologist's laboratory.

A huge array of hardware and training designs now confronts the somewhat ill-prepared training director. In his resentment, he calls some of these devices gimmicks. He feels he ought somehow to be buying and innovating; but in which direction? And how shall he justify what he buys? Certainly he has greatly improved his potential status by taking on tasks of high corporate priority, by building external allegiance to associations of other training managers, and by using the increasingly potent technology available to him. But that status is still potential; the training manager has before him the ingredients necessary for full acceptance, but he has yet to assemble them.

Training Trends in Other Countries

The status problems experienced by the American training manager are shared by his European counterparts. It is difficult, in European and British firms, for a training manager to obtain the funds and backing necessary for large-scale manpower programs and management training. In England it was necessary to legislate for training. Each company, according to the British Industrial Training Act (1964),[59] was *required* to train and to invest in it.

Something of the attitude of British training managers, given these conditions of mandatory training is conveyed by the report of Frederick Lippert,[60] who visited a program for training officers at the Bath University School of Technology: ". . . intense, dedicated, and bewildered by a plethora of programs, concepts, and procedures, some of which smell strongly of gimmickry to them." [p. 8] These men were suspicious of American dependence on social science and a bit skeptical of management-training techniques. It would appear that these British trainers were expressing many of the attitudes of American trainers just a few years earlier.

Eastern European countries have moved drastically to join the manpower-training movement, even including, to the surprise of some, management training. Romania has written a training act like the British, and President Ceausescu said in 1969: "Let us organize management training programs to help managers know and understand the new ways in which they should carry out their activities. . . . We cannot . . . accept improvisation. There is a need for thorough training." [p. 5] [61] ("Improvisation" refers to the traditional line-manager's approach to training—late, informal, and unsystematic. The new training attitudes insist on planned, professionally organized, and systematic training.) The extension of the training concept to management in Communist countries is especially interesting. H. E. Frank [61] (Bath University School of Technology) has predicted the establishment of management-development centers in most Eastern European countries. Each would be authorized and operated by the state. He sees this as a logical result of the move, in Communist countries, away from belief in sheer quantity production and toward a more consumer-oriented point of view. Again, the evolution toward an environmentally responsive management is so clear that even the Communist Party recognizes it.

An early result of this trend is a move toward greater importance for training; but the European and British training managers will eventually find, if our American experience is a guide, that abundant technology and higher-priority assignments (such as management training) are not enough. The training manager will find, in Europe as in the United States, that he is handed immense responsibility for changing manpower skills and attitudes, but not the resources necessary. Why not?

NEW TECHNICAL RESOURCES
AND THEIR DANGERS

When managers acquire new tools, like boys with toys, they naturally are enthusiastic. When one has a gun, he wants to shoot it; when he buys a tool, he wants to start using it. Managers are especially impressed by new hardware such as computers. It even seems possible that the fastest way to install sophisticated training programs in some companies might be to build them into a computer. The computer costs a million dollars, and the training software could have been installed for much less. But it just wouldn't look impressive.

Eastern European governments have, perhaps for this reason, run pell-mell toward heavy purchasing of electronic data-processing equipment for use in training. In the fifties and sixties a similar attitude in the United States led to building (and vastly overproducing) teaching machines for industry and education long before there was sufficient software (or learning programs) to put into the machines.

The problem is not the machines (who can doubt the immense potential of computer-aided instruction?) but the overvaluation of machines alone. The error in buying physical tools for training lies not in the tools themselves, but in believing that those tools can substitute for training. The result is rather like shipping quantities of scalpels, drugs, and operating-room fixtures to countries with no surgeons (that's been done, too!).

Clearly a second influence on the training manager's style is the competition to entrepreneurial thinking offered by the narrowly technocratic approach of management. (By technocratic, I mean specifically the attempt to use tools without using the *concepts* of technology.) There are, for example, engineering schools of two kinds. The one kind teaches the student to work with things and materials and capitalizes on the natural interest of many students in the concreteness of nature. The other kind teaches the student to begin with people's design problems and to exploit the assets of things and materials in carrying out these designs. The second school teaches students to think, reason, and apply logic as well as to understand human needs. It is closer to liberal education.

Narrowly technocratic management uses the first approach. It values material things because they are concrete. It is impressed by what *things* can do (for example, the wonder of video tape playback) rather than whether they are doing anything worth doing. Such management undervalues knowledge of human nature and regards software as less impressive than hardware. In particular, it eschews the behavioral sciences as lacking in predictive power (which is *not* true) and as being more abstract than concrete (not true, either). Here we note a curious attitude. Nothing would seem to be more concrete than a particular person, a human being. The physical technologist has people around him all his life. Their behavior is real, tangible, and a major part of his reality. But he will pretend—he has been so educated by his technical background—that human reality to him is a less solid reality than that of material things. The technocratic manager then, when

Technocratic design questions	Humanistic design questions
1. Men and machines are alternatives to one another. Normally, a machine is a cheaper and more reliable substitute. Thus,what machine can replace the unreliable and expensive trainer?	1. Physical tools are viewed as an extension of human characteristics, not vice versa. Hence, how can the energies of people be freed through machine extensions?
2. A training program is a straight-line sequence of changes in which the trainee is progressively modified, like a piece of raw material. What are the logical steps of training, from start (raw material) to end (finished product)?	2. A training program is a reorganization of human energies, i.e., of motivated skills. What incentives to learn are provided by the training? What skills are to be improved?
3. Does the program adequately exploit the available hardware — e.g., computers, video tape playback, electronic devices, slide projectors, etc.?	3. Is hardware integrated into the design where actually needed? Does it support, rather than dominate, the training?

Figure 7.2

he is given funds to develop a training program, finds it more congenial to purchase equipment, space, or off-the-shelf programs. Then he operates the program. It is an attitude which some would consider peculiarly American; now, however, we see it popping up among British and East European training managers. Figure 7.2 contrasts technocracy with a more humanistic view of training.

Behavioral Technology:
A New Resource

The latest nonhumanistic technology available to training managers treats human behavior as a thing and reshapes it for productive purposes. However one may be offended by the moral assumptions of behavioral technologists (and I am), their methods *do* work. What are those assumptions; what is the new power it places in the hands of training designers; and what reservations have we about it?

Behavioral technology—or to use another name, "behavioral modification"—is the change of human behavior by applying conditioning principles. "Conditioning" here refers to the rather elaborate body of laboratory-tested knowledge of how animal and human behavior can be changed by judicious use of rewards and penalties. The classic design is well known: give a dog food immediately after a bell, and he will eventually salivate when he hears the bell. The newer conditioning design is not so well known: give the dog food only if he raises his right foot while wagging his tail, and he will eventually do these things in order to get the food. The food is a "reinforcement" for foot-raising and tail-wagging, and the newer conditioning is called, by some, "reinforcement conditioning."

Programmed instruction (for example, teaching machines) is an application of the dozen or so established principles of reinforcement conditioning. The program is essentially simple: ask a child to give his answer to an arithmetic problem, and then immediately confirm it when correct; in this way, one reinforces the most salient or recent aspects of his arithmetic reasoning. Give him the answer an hour later, and he couldn't care less; little or nothing is stamped in. Using such principles, behavioral technologists have taught pigeons to play Ping Pong and steer torpedoes; turkeys to play box hockey on exhibition at county fairs; speech-blocked children to speak; catatonic (or grossly out-of-contact) patients to rise from their stupor. The important point to note here is that behavioral technology *works.*

Like physical technology, however, behavioral technology's great powers also contain dangers. In general, these resemble the similar dangers of physical technology: overuse—the training manager may lean too much on behavioral-modification programs.

To state this differently, he may attempt to develop reinforcement programs which are not related to the corporate goals or to the human situation in which they are used.

A psychologist once attempted to install programmed instruction in a school of medicine, and its effects are certainly instructive. His error was a classical one. Because he did not explain the purpose of the programmed instruction to faculty and students and did not let them participate in designing and implementing the program, they rejected it. Medical students said things like:

- "This program treats us like robots. We'll show the guy we aren't. We won't bother with his stupid program."
- "This program is based on animal experiments. Physicians are not animals. We won't do the program."
- "The faculty has lost interest in teaching us and is turning us over to the teaching machines. That's not what we pay tuition for."

In brief, the behavioral-technology program may have been well designed, but was not put into the humanistic context within which a wise manager will define his work. That suggests a third new resource for training managers.

Humanistic Psychology: Its Power and Limitations

One of the innovations in American training methods which has excited the greatest interest (and concern) has been the use of "sensitivity training groups" (also known as "T groups," "encounter groups," and other names, all suggesting the application of group dynamics techniques) pioneered by German social psychologist Kurt Lewin. T groups have had a stormy career. "Trainers" vary greatly in their qualifications, and some companies have been clumsy in their manner of enrolling employees and managers in these programs. Since the experience of a T group is an intensive one, some emotional damage has perhaps been done.

As even a person who has been through a T group has some difficulty in explaining what it is, training managers as a whole can reasonably be expected to vary in their opinions of the technique's worth. My own view is that T groups are not training at all in the sense in which training has been used in this chapter. Neither are they psychotherapy; a person who is emotionally ill should not enter a T group. Some would call T groups educational; this is a misnomer since there are no prerequisite courses, no reading, no content to speak of, and the aims are more deeply personal than most educators would understand. The best term for T groups, in my opinion, is "growth experience." They provide an opportunity for managers to "grow up" in their interpersonal relations. The limitations of T groups seem to be these:

1. They are not training, in that before-and-after determinations of performance are not a required aspect of the experience. This means that a manager is hard put to say what was obtained for the investment in time and money.

2. If T groups are not really training programs, then training departments would not appear the logical place to administer them. But there is not, in most corporations, any other department which is better suited to select, evaluate, and provide liaison with T-group trainers ("NTL Associates," as they are called, are only rarely on corporate payrolls and are thus usually brought in as consultants).

3. While the T group does provide a plausible claim to offer a growth experience in human relations, the managers who need it most cannot really profit much from it; the childish, infantile, neurotic, or autocratic manager who causes so many difficulties in a corporation (in other words the very person who needs the program the most) should not enter the T group for emotional reasons.

Some offshoots of a T group, however, do appear to offer a number of promising dividends which bypass these limitations. For example, when I train managers to select and promote people, I begin that training with a brief T group and then move on to the formal training. This technique has the effect of creating an open climate for learning.

The Self-sealing Role of Expert

What happens, then, to the expert has been illustrated by computers, programmed instruction, and T groups. He observes, learns, and masters a new technique. The effort required may be great, the investment great, and the inherent fascination great. He becomes something more than a specialist; he becomes an enthusiast, even a cultist.

In such a way, the training manager who acquires these new resources and masters their use becomes a victim of his own success. The techniques are so potent—or promise to be so potent—that he loses contact with the managerial role itself. This is all right if he knows that he is doing it and intends to. But learning to manage is itself so complex that one wonders whether it is possible to become a top manager and also an expert. He should make a choice and live with the consequences.

What this suggests about technical careers is that they compete with the development of general managers and draw off talent that ought to flow into the entrepreneurial levels of Bois's [62] evolutionary scale. This is recognized explicitly in the pay scales of some R&D firms, who have two ladders: one for the technical men, within their specialty; one for the general-management men. It is possible in some heavily technical organizations (such as hospitals) for the specialists to earn more than the generalist.

LEARNING GENERAL MANAGEMENT WITHIN A SPECIALTY

The dilemma for a corporation is this: each department is relatively specialized but yet must develop managers who have the overview. How is this possible? How can the self-sealing expert trap be avoided?

It is not so simple as rotating young men through different departments, a solution Clarence Randall developed at Inland Steel. This cannot always be done. As the number of technical specialties proliferates it becomes impossible to rotate a man through everything. After all, it takes him a while to learn the department's operations. Rotation could become a mere exercise in superficiality.

Here's the suggestion: professionalize every department; create as many environmental interfaces as possible in it; and recast it in the entrepreneurial mold as much as possible. In theory, such a department—no matter how specialized— would become a suitable breeding ground for general managers. Let's see how this suggestion works out in the case of training departments.

Recasting Training
in the Entrepreneurial Mold

The training director's problem is to learn to use his resources in an entrepreneurial way. There appear to be three things he can do:

- emphasize the evaluation of training
- learn to manage the training process
- humanize training

First, consider the relative status of marketing in the corporation. Not long ago, marketing departments had to fight their way into the executive suite. They were specialists, too, just like the training man. They had to contend with older business functions—finance, production, even law—and as a newcomer were regarded with slight condescension. Even though the marketing department suffered all the traditional difficulties of being defined as staff, it escaped in large measure those narrow bounds.

Why was it possible for marketing and has not yet happened for the training function? Marketing has a formidable and perhaps decisive advantage: contact with the customer—interface with the single most significant part of the environment. True, it is sometimes possible for some training departments to develop this interface—at IBM, the customers are trained to use the equipment, and sales simply would have been impossible without it.

But, generally speaking, the marketing, merchandising, and sales people interface with the environment, and the training department does not (except through professional associations). This is one of the prime distinctions between bureaucratic and entrepreneurial management. Is it therefore an impossible obstacle for the training department or for any other specialized staff service which cannot deal with the environment?

What all such departments can do, even if they are not in contact with the firm's customers, is to adopt a results-oriented approach to training. This is increasingly the orientation of training departments.

Fostering Results-oriented Training Policies

Results-oriented management in the case of the training department calls for stating the objectives in advance and then measuring their achievement. To be entrepreneurial in style, the objectives should be connected with the overall purposes of the firm or, at the very least, should be stated in terms of relevant performance over which the training manager does not have *direct* control.

That is, the training program's objectives must be stated in terms of trainees' on-the-job performances. The objectives should not be stated in terms of favorable ratings from the trainees, although trainee opinion is not irrelevant. Any seasoned training manager knows this is difficult. One would suppose that he would receive valuable help in the design and subsequent evaluation of training. But until the late sixties he had not much help in published models of any sophistication.

Is it any wonder that so many training programs are simply borrowed by one company from another? The question asked by most training directors about a proposed new program is not whether there is proof that it works but "Who else uses it?" This is hardly an entrepreneurial way of thinking. It would be like producing a machine not because it is selling well but because other companies are producing it. The training manager needs an index such as sales volume so that he can measure the effectiveness of his programs.

It is perhaps easiest to document the lack of serious evaluation in the federal training effort. Several hundred millions are expended every year on the training of federal employees. According to testimony before the Congress,[9] only very minor effort goes into the evaluation of such programs.

Again, one may emphatically *not* evaluate a program merely by asking the participants how they liked it. This would be akin to testing a new product by inquiring whether customers said they liked it, ignoring the critical question of whether they *bought* it and *repurchased* it.

Evaluation appears to be the principal difference between marketing and personnel administration. Marketing,* by definition, is in touch with the outer environment, is compelled to ask questions about the use of its products by people outside the firm. Personnel administration, in contact primarily with employees of the firm, is not inclined by the nature of its work to measure its results against any environmental criteria.

Recall, in an earlier chapter, that one of the critical differences noted between bureaucratic and entrepreneurial orienta-

---

* Among the exceptions to this statement would be personnel departments engaged heavily in labor relations, recruiting, vestibule training, public relations, or research, all of which can be ways of interfacing with a significant part of the business environment.

tions lay in this very interest in the environment. The bureaucrat is only interested in the policies and procedures of his own firm and in its inner workings. The entrepreneur, by contrast, is primarily interested in the relation of his firm to the outer world because it is *outside* the firm that the opportunities lie. He subjects his ideas to further tests.

It is thus only by a difficult struggle that the personnel department can avoid being bureaucratized. The training function, perhaps, has a better chance of avoiding it: the training program, being of short duration in many instances, can more easily permit before-and-after evaluation to be taken. This is not so true of many other personnel functions. Training, at least, ought to ask Peter Drucker's question: How do we measure a training program for its ability to achieve results? Sometimes the results are cost reduction. It is without a doubt easily documented that many training programs do reduce costs or increase sales. But one cannot determine the training consequences of T groups in this manner or even the effects of excellent simulation training, such as the Kepner-Tregoe.[63] And yet one must still evaluate those programs.

Thus evaluation against costs is not always possible, but there are other kinds of evaluation. For example, one can show that after a Kepner-Tregoe training program, most managers seem to know what they are doing when they conduct departmental meetings; the meetings are better designed after than before the training. One might determine a cost reduction showing the value of this improvement, but this cost would not really express its true value.

Managing Training

A training manager in the entrepreneurial style should spend less time and energy on operating his program; he would invest more time thinking through what it is supposed to do and on gathering data to be sure that the program does, in fact, do those things.

The enterprise of training is devoted to changing human behavior, skills, and attitudes. The risks of training lie in being open, in advance, about the fact that there will be a hard-nosed evaluation afterward. The marketing manager who puts a new product line on the market takes a risk when he does so; his failures are going to be as loud as his successes. This is a principal reason for paying marketing managers more than traditional training managers and for promoting them more frequently to the highest levels of the corporation.

Manpower and management training are as close to the essential operations of a large organization as is marketing. But it will not excite the admiration or provoke the respect of the rest of the organization until the training manager is willing to stick his neck out by stating, in advance, what a program will accomplish and then by permitting a public audit which shows whether or not the program actually did it.

The training manager who operates the classical cycle of planning, implementing, and evaluating *is* a general manager. There is no reason that experience in being a general manager in the training field is not as useful a background for the chief executive as being a general manager in any other area of the corporation's work.

The Problem of "Managerial Machismo"

One difference between the training department and departments which work primarily with things is its greater technical base in the behavioral sciences. This leads, in some companies, to some problems of conflict with the stereotype of "the manager."

"The manager," as Miner [44] showed with his research, is defined by some as a sort of super male, a "hard-nosed," tough-minded, decisive power figure. He knows about hard things such as money, machines, markets, but not about soft things such as feelings, attitudes, and, in general, the human side of management. Or if he knows about the softer side of management life, he does not permit it to influence him too much. The big decisions of what is best for the company, in this view, cannot be made properly if the general manager permits himself to be unduly swayed away from the "facts." And facts are assumed to be about hard things; feelings and attitudes are not facts. Don't be too gentle; to be a strong manager is to avoid sentimentality and soft-headedness. These views are badly in error.

Anyone who has participated in a T group knows that much of the interaction taking place is anything but gentle. The difficulty with T groups is precisely that somebody gets hurt emotionally. It is a rough kind of training. The brutality of encounter and T groups can occur at the very point at which the super-masculine manager says sentimentality exists: the point at which the group talks frankly about feelings and emotions. This most humanistic of all training is also the roughest of all training experience for some participants. Equating humanistic attitudes with sentimentality is a gross misstatement. It is one of the prejudices training managers must face and overcome.

The reasons go far beyond the status of training in the corporation. The idea of "managerial *machismo*"—be a big strong male and run the corporation—has also resulted in some dangerous distortions in managerial perspective. Two examples come to mind.

■ In attempting to sell a morale survey, consultants run into sales resistance from high-machismo managers who literally do not want to know what employees are saying about them. No guts.

■ Blindness to human facts is at times so great as to produce skepticism about saving money by attention to human facts. I remember a plant which had a turnover rate among production workers of nearly 100 percent a year. The costs of recruiting, training, and social security benefits were totalling in out-of-pocket costs (not theoretical costs) of nearly a quarter of a million dollars a year. The plant manager responsible for the policies which produced the turnover seemed to be totally uninterested in the potential saving. However, he was very interested in the savings he could obtain by buying new equipment or by increasing his sales.

In Europe, I once participated in a management seminar for European managers, most of whom had never heard a lecture from a behavioral scientist. They were alert, polite, and quick. However, in the same seminar, they heard lectures from general managers and an engineer. In writing up the seminars, some participants attributed a conflict to the speakers which did not exist.

■ To the behavioral scientists they attributed the attitude that people come before profits and that one should be courteous, kindly, and careful in his human relations.

■ To the general managers, they attributed the attitude that profits come first, and people be damned.

The amusing fact was that one of the general managers and the engineer happen to be among the most humanistic in attitudes toward business of any managers I have ever known. The participants' illusion was largely the projection of their own *machismo*. Whether this is characteristic of European managers I could not say. It is in any event a dangerous attitude and certainly a distortion of what the behavioral scientists had to say.

MANAGING TRAINING IN THE ENTREPRENEURIAL STYLE

The training manager became a specialist after World War II, turning increasingly to the knowledge base provided him by the behavioral sciences. This brought in increasingly powerful resources and tools for him but could not solve the semantic problems of being defined as staff, which is an absurd notion about him but is a historical definition of the field. He further could not avoid the bureaucratizing influence of personnel departments. The frustrations of the field result from these trends.

They especially result from the contradictions between the technocratic view of the corporation (which is that the manager's job is to acquire and use specialized tools—both software and hardware) and the professional and entrepreneurial views. The training manager has the dilemma between being a powerful (but limited) specialist—and reaching beyond his techniques to learn general management skills. It is a mistake for him to think that those skills are learned only in positions which are commonly labeled general management, although it is true that the prejudices of corporations are accurately mirrored in the practices of labeling some jobs as line and others as staff. It is possible to be a generalist in training management; whether the training manager can persuade others that this is what he is, is another matter.

Even if he acquires generalist skills, there are subtle barriers between the training manager and the entrepreneurial role. That role is based on an attitude of what business is—risk taking in a futuristic, environmentally oriented, managerial sense. The barrier can be breached by any manager who develops the capacity to form economically rational visions of the future. This is what entrepreneurs do that most people cannot or will not do.

chapter eight

Choosing Managers

In Lewis Strauss's memoirs [64] he reviews a number of the most significant decisions he made as head of the Atomic Energy Commission. The list includes technical decisions, which one would expect, but also a large number which deal with people —especially the key appointments and removals he made or influenced. I would venture that almost any chief executive would confirm this experience of Admiral Strauss—that at least half the major decisions concern the appointment, assignment, reorganization of duties, or removal of key people. This is precisely the kind of decision regarding which there is least help in books on decision making and in computer aids to decision.

How professional and entrepreneurial managers make decisions about people is the question of this chapter. It is obviously a critically important question for the future of the business firm. Let the reader also reflect on the chances he may fall victim to a badly designed management-selection process. He might be well advised to improve it before that day comes!

The question of how managers are, and should be, selected is full of paradoxes. One has already been mentioned—if the decision regarding the next president (or other key executive) is so important, why does decision-making theory never discuss it? Also consider these puzzles:

- If the performance of line managers is so highly visible and public, since it is a matter of economic performance, and if the man who gets the best results ought to be promoted, why is the choice of a president a difficult choice?
- Why is it that the least objective and most unreliable selection procedure (the interview) is the one most widely used?

The confusions suggested by these paradoxes are a good index to the current state of manager selection. It is, in brief, an odd mixture of objectivity, subjectivity, politics, bad logic, and injustice. Perhaps it is not so serious as in Peter's principle [65] that in the corporation each rises to the highest level of his incompetence. But it is serious enough to ask some painful questions about.

The confusion and paradoxes are due to the intermingling of at least four separate theories or systems. In the "political" system, the manager (or other key person) is chosen for the job intuitively, the decision based on his influence or power. This is the oldest of all selection systems. In the "bureaucratic" system, the manager is chosen objectively, the decision based on rules which are established by political means or by arbitrary directive from the top management level. In the "technocratic" system, the manager is chosen objectively, the decision based on procedures (especially tests) having a known scientific basis. This is the newest of all selection systems. In the "entrepreneurial" system, the manager is chosen intuitively, the decision based on subjective estimates of his ability to carry out a particular plan or operate a particular firm.

In spite of the confusion, business is probably no worse off than the processes of filling key posts in government and the military. Business probably is much better off than the university or the church,* wherein the selection systems are almost totally archaic. But let us not take time for complacency; the situation is bad enough in business. It is always unjust when good men are passed by for promotion because of a decision maker's ignorance, bad logic, or sloth.

The oldest system of all—the political—is still very much with us. Anthony Jay [30] reminds us that political realism must guide our understanding of corporate management. The executive career has long been and still is founded on the arts of acquiring power, connections, and influence. Nor is this totally without logic. Prestige in a well-run business firm, for example, is to some extent based on who obtains results; and prestige is one of the major factors used in political arithmetic. But the way in which political sums are arrived at is much more obscure than is commonly described in the textbooks on personnel selection. The immense gulf between theory and practice is nowhere better documented than in a recent study in which Glickman, Hahn, Fleishman, and Baxter [67] interviewed a number of executives in thirteen corporations. They asked these executives about recently appointed managers and the manner in which the appointments were decided upon. In general, they found that:

■ Top management selection is not like the selection process at lower echelons.

■ Decisions are made by highly informal methods, in small, intimate groups.

* Professors are selected to teach on the basis of the writing they have done.[66] Candidates for the ministry are selected by a mysterious process which is quite beyond my ken.

■ Decisions are based on highly personal assessments of data collected through direct observation.

In some firms, the viciousness of infighting to gain higher appointments is too much for some to stomach. Thus the quiet, more rational, and seemingly more professional style of the bureaucrat has its appeals. The impartiality of bureaucratic rules (such a rule as "Every manager who is in line for a promotion must be informed of the reasons he did not get it") at least intends to provide a safeguard against arbitrary political excess. The principal feature in the bureaucratic approach, however, is to formulate rules which specify qualifications for jobs. Beginning in the federal government in the nineteenth century, and slowly moving into the states, the military, and industry, bureaucratic selection now challenges the old power plays. We will examine whether this challenge is what it seems, and whether it can produce what it promises.

THE ANATOMY OF CHOICE

The logic underlying all selection systems is fundamentally the same: to collect data, appraise it, compare it with corporate requirements or plans, and make a decision. The different systems, however, apply this logic differently to the problem.

Before comparing them, we first examine the fundamental nature of personal data. From this examination we will suggest a universal or ideal model to follow. This ideal model will help us choose features from the different systems in proceeding to design one which is fair to both the aspirants for top jobs and to the corporation which needs human excellence in those jobs.

What Is a Good Decision?

A good decision, from the corporation's standpoint, is one which has favorable consequences. In particular, a good choice of an executive is later considered good if the job goes well. However, it is not easy to prove, in the case of poor performance, that it was a lack in the man accountable; it may be that the corporation gave him insufficient resources.

A good decision from the individual's standpoint is one which is based on certain favorable data from his career. Ordinarily he considers that he is as good as his previous *peak* performance. The miler defines himself as a "four-minute miler" if he has broken that barrier even once; although his average may actually be 4:06, he will not conclude that this is his level. A person will usually equate his proper salary level to his peak previous earnings. He will not average in the bad years.

This emphasis on peak performance is not illogical. A man cannot run a four-minute mile by accident. No one writes an accidental symphony or a Nobel-Prize winning novel by chance. If one achieves, he has ability.

On the other hand, there are many possible factors which induce a failure, and they are not all under the person's control. Sonny Jurgensen can hardly be faulted because the Redskins did not win most of their games. A success depends on many factors, all of which must be present (including ability). Thus one cannot be sure which of these many factors caused the failure. Consider a chain when it breaks in the dark. We cannot tell which link is broken, but when it holds, we can be sure all links are whole.

Fortunately, the two concepts (the company's versus the individual's) of a good decision do not totally conflict. In predicting human performance, the best way to make a decision having favorable consequences is to consider evidence from the past performance.

Since a good decision for the corporation is one which has good consequences, this means that selection decisions must on the average *predict* consequences. Accuracy in such prediction is in the interest of the individual aspirant; if there is good evidence that he will fail on a job, surely this evidence is in his interest, and surely it is not in his interest to be considered for a job at which he will likely fail.

When we talk about prediction, we are talking probability (unless one wishes to advocate tea leaves, astrology, or secret intimations, these systems of prediction we will ignore). All decisions are probabilistic statements about the future, at least by implication. Two investments may have the same payoff but with different probabilities. This makes the choice easy. Two candidates for an executive position should also be considered alternative investments. That is, there is a risk element. It is at least as large as the executive's compensation; really, many times larger than this.

Now, there are some who would deny that probability statements can be made about which executive will perform better. They doubt predictions can be made, in the first place, and suggest that they *should* not be made in the second place—it does not seem humanistic. These arguments can be quickly disposed of. No one claims that executive performance is exactly predictable, and it is necessary only that probability estimates be better than guessing to make them useful. Logically, if no estimates of consequences of a decision can be made, the decision cannot be responsibly made at all. As for the humanistic argument, one is persuaded that it is valid, but the argument should guide us in the *way* key posts are filled—not prevent us from filling them rationally. It would seem eminently humanistic to fill top posts with men who will help corporations survive, who will not make terrible military miscalculations, or who will not impose ineffective laws on us.

Are predictions of executive performance more accurate than guessing? First, try to imagine a society in which behavior was random. No one would stop at red lights, serve meals on time, or meet his obligations. Prediction is inherent in our very concept of a social order and still more in our concept of a corporation. Second, there is factual evidence that executives do perform as they are predicted.* Executive selection is not a game of Russian roulette.

But *how* are predictions best made about executive performance? Aye, there's the rub. The different systems pose and therefore answer this question in different ways. The technologists, those who construct and use standardized devices for selection, for a long time had the only system which checked its own predictions. Thus there have not been many comparisons of the effectiveness of, let us say, testing versus bureaucratic standards.

The Life-history Model of Assessment

Going further in the task of constructing an ideal model, consider now the common element in almost all assessment systems: the use of data about the person's past performance. Let us consider assessment as a general process in our society. A person undergoes assessment at several critical points in his life:

- in school
- before admission to college
- during recruiting for his first job with a corporation
- at successive intervals during consideration for higher posts if he progresses
- if and when he becomes ill, his condition is assessed by a medical diagnostician

* In Meyer,[68] the results of several large corporate managerial-selection studies were reported. Laurent described a Standard Oil (New Jersey) study of 443 managers over several years, after they were evaluated with a test battery. There is little question that the intelligence test, personality inventory, and biography survey produced valid predictions. Kolb repeated this study at Humble, where the methods were not only found effective, but apparently their effectiveness increased with time. The methods used at Sears were also reviewed by Bentz in this book, with especially good results from the biographic questionnaire; on this point, see discussion of the life-history model (pp. 159–165).

■ if and when he should become accused of a crime, a jury will review evidence about him

■ if he tries to raise funds or obtain large loans, his history will be reviewed in some detail

■ if he runs for political office, the voters will consider his "record"

What all these assessment points have in common is that some responsible official or professional looks at data about a person and makes a decision having a bearing on his future. The basic rationale guiding the ways in which the data are collected, analyzed, and used to make the decision constitutes a "theory of assessment." For reasons I have presented in another book,[69] the most sensible approach to understand assessment is to view it from the standpoint of the person's life history. The data are about the person's life; the analysis is a matter of common sense (rather than a technical problem); and the decision is based on estimates of the future which grow out of an understanding of the person's past. When assessment is defined in this manner, it has proven possible to measure (by using cases with known outcomes) what kinds of officials or professionals can in fact make accurate estimates of the person's future behavior. Among the findings from this research are these:

■ Persons untrained in the fields of psychology or personnel selection can make predictions of life-history events (it *does* appear to be a matter of common sense).

■ Some persons are consistently better at making such predictions than are others (not every manager possesses this "common sense").

■ It is possible to train assessment officials to make better life-history predictions.

In life-history assessment, we do not "test" the applicant so much as we collect data about his past history. The application blank is of key importance in this system, and this seems to be a universal practice in personnel administration. However, at the executive level, when the decisions are so much more complex, it would seem that a far more searching investigation of his past career would be in order. It is, in effect, necessary to write a case about an applicant for a key post. If the case is comprehensive, accurate, fully understood, and contains data relevant to the position the man is being considered for, the predictions of his performance have the best chance of being accurate.*

Why can predictions be made at all? This question is answered in different ways by different systems of assessment. For example, it is the view of some industrial psychologists that predictions can be made from tests because human behavior obeys certain laws, and testing takes advantage of this lawfulness in making valid forecasts of future performance. However, my own view is more like that of Alfred Adler. The principal reason we can predict performance is either intention (the person now expresses an intention which he later carries out) or consistency (a person develops a unified style of life to which he adheres). We study his past history in order to find out what he is trying to do (his intentions or motivations) and to learn his *modus operandi* (his style of life or characteristic way of carrying out his intentions).

One of the problems of choosing managers is that we are often making a prediction about how the manager will perform in a new situation, different from those about which we have past-performance data. We would expect prediction of performance after promotion to be less accurate than predic-

* One should avoid being glib about this. "Writing a case" is a serious discipline, requiring both tough-minded investigation of facts and some sensitivity to human factors. In spite of some decades of emphasis on case methods in schools of business, very little has been written down about how cases are prepared. Hence, when it is suggested that executive appraisal requires case writing, no one should think it any more simple and easy than constructing a new psychological test would be.

tion of performance on the present job. And yet it is the performance after promotion which is the more important question.

This prediction is so difficult that we do a number of things to hedge the bet. One is to collect enough data on the person to ensure that the prediction is based on the largest possible amount of information. The more vital the job, the more such information ought to be collected. This policy assumes that intuitive prediction is on the whole more accurate if we have more data. Although some have disputed this assumption, my own data support it.[69] Another hedge is to minimize wishful thinking—making optimistic predictions because we like the guy—by having strangers make the prediction. Companies sometimes ask for consultant opinion before making a promotion. However, the consultant normally has observed the candidate for a brief period, and the company logically should not hesitate to overrule his judgment in cases in which they believe their data are more complete.

The Phases of Assessment

All assessment systems put the person through a series of stages of consideration. In the life-history assessment system, the stages are approached in the following manner:

1. Data collection: a very detailed career and personal history is assembled; the more complex the position, the more detail.

2. Analysis of data: these data are critically evaluated to establish which parts are more factual and significant; these more factual and significant data suggest a certain pattern of abilities and motivations; when the pattern matches the apparent requirements of the position, the evaluation is favorable.

3. Prediction: the assessment official makes a series of specific predictions regarding how well the applicant will handle the key situations likely to arise in the job. This is the point

at which the probability factor enters into the assessment process.

4. Decision: the final decision is based on a combination of the probabilities of effectiveness in performance. The concept here is that of "utility"—probability times "desirability" of outcome.*

5. Follow-up: the accuracy of estimate should be checked against the subsequent records of the man's performance, ideally, whether he is promoted or not. When this follow-up information is given as feedback to the assessment official, he has a chance of improving his future decision making.

In the life-history research reported elsewhere,[69] my colleagues and I found that when such results are provided as feedback to managers, they improve in making predictions, and therefore in decision making.

The Logic of Life-
history Assessment

In brief, then, this assessment model holds that all decisions should be based on evidence from the past. It does not hold that the past history limits what a person can do in the future, but rather provides clues as to the major directions his career history is taking. It provides such clues because people reveal their intentions and have a *modus operandi* which can be seen in the way they perform their jobs.

The logic is that of using known performance to estimate potential performance. This logic is not new; it is used to scout football players, to seed tennis stars, and to pick horses.

---

*Suppose a manager has five duties, but each duty has a relative importance (or "desirability") factor. Thus the favorable prediction on each duty should be weighted by its desirability. The total evaluation should in some way combine probability and desirability factors. In Utility Theory, this total evaluation would compute a score for each duty, where $U = $ Probability $\times$ Desirability, and sum the scores for the duties. While there has been no little research in such utility measurement, it has not, to my knowledge, been studied in the present problem.[70]

But the application of this logic is broader than in judging specific talent. In the area of manager assessment, it virtually calls for a biography on any serious contender for a high position.

The Problem of
Invasion of Privacy

Some believe such a biography ought to be restricted to career facts. In bureaucratic systems, there is pressure toward such restriction. There was a big flap at the State Department in the sixties when a woman candidate for overseas assignment complained that she was being questioned about her sex life. Congressmen demanded to know what right the State Department had to this information and doubted that it had any connection to diplomacy anyway. Old hands snickered in private (everyone knew the liabilities of affair-prone consulate staff), while in public they solemnly declared that prurient curiosity must be kept out of personnel screening.

The reader knows that the underground and backstage life of executives has significance. Just as one is entitled to learn of an applicant's gambling debts before hiring him as a bank teller, there is a wide range of emotional, financial, business involvements a person might have which would affect his objectivity and effectiveness in a particular executive post. The purpose of such inquiry is not to detect a person's private malefactions and malfeasances; knowing the ways in which an applicant is a "swinger" is not designed to denigrate him but rather to see him in the three-dimensional way required for an honest estimate of the kind of flesh-and-blood executive he will likely make.

The principle is that the more vital the post, the less entitled to privacy is the candidate. The principle runs headlong against the principle of the right to privacy. One common resolution of this conflict is to use outside consultants, whose integrity is established, to act as intermediaries. They should know all, but need pass on only an opinion as to the probable effectiveness of the candidate. The room for abuse of the principles is very large. Something like the legal concept of "due process" should be eventually devised to find compromises between the rights of the company to know and the right of the applicant to privacy.

TRENDS IN EXECUTIVE SELECTION

In my judgment, the life-history assessment model is ultimately the model most applicable to the appraisal of managers, especially when professional and entrepreneurial executives participate in the appraisal process.* However, this is not the prevailing approach at the present time.

The four broad systems, defined earlier, operate on different assumptions. They have different purposes, methods, and collect data in different ways. These are shown in Figure 8.1.

The recent trend, in my opinion, has been toward the technical system, especially in light of the important evidence reported by several large companies in recent years. Advocates of this system, primarily utilizing objective tests and personality inventories to measure the person's characteristics, tend to be critical of subjective data-gathering techniques such as the interview. Dunnette and Bass [71] have said of the interview that it is ". . . the most widely used method for selecting employees, despite the fact that it is a costly, inefficient, and usually invalid procedure." [p. 337]

It is worth asking why the interview is used so much if there are rational arguments against it. First, there is no real way to understand life history from a mere "cold record" of facts; it is commonly recognized in personnel administration that one has to be able to cross-examine a person to locate and

---

*AT&T is an important example. The "assessment-center" concept pioneered and developed there calls for assessment of a manager by his peers.

Comparative Analysis of Four Systems of Decision Making

Common Problem: what use is made of what kinds of data from the candidate's past history to decide his qualifications?

Question	Political system	Bureaucratic system	Technologic system	Entrepreneurial system
Definition:	Intuitive choice based on influence or power.	Objective choice based on rules established by power.	Objective choice based on procedures having scientific foundation.	Intuitive choice based on data about past performance in similar situations.
Purpose:	Preserve power and group solidarity.	Correct autocratic excess of political system, reduce costs.	Improve accuracy by analysis of past decisions.	Maximize the chances of success of the operation.
Rationale for human performance:	People will do on the job what they must do.	People will do what they should do.	People adhere to behavioral laws.	People are likely to behave in accordance with the goals they set.
Basic data required:	Impressionistic, intuitive data.	Standardized data — qualifications.	Standardized data — tests and other quantitative data.	Impressionistic, intuitive data; ideally, cases are prepared.
Prediction:	None made.	None made.	Objective.	Intuitive.
Follow-through to check accuracy:	None made, since no prediction was made.	None made, since no prediction was made.	Essential to the validation of tests.	A natural part of the managerial process.

Figure 8.1

interpret the inevitable obscurities and contradictions in such data. It is felt by many psychologists and psychiatrists that a person's history cannot be understood properly without also knowing how the person himself evaluates each of its major events. There is no way to cross-examine a person or to learn how he evaluates his own background data without an interview.

There is also an ethical case for interviewing. The tradition, in Western ethics, is that one ought to be able to confront those who make judgments about him (for example, his accusers in a court of law). It does not seem right to make decisions which determine a person's entire future without an opportunity for him to interrogate those who make such decisions and to present his own case to his own satisfaction. Something like this ethical position led to a feeling of moral outrage at the recent newsstory reporting that Howard Hughes had had one of his chief executives fired. Few personnel men would countenance "third-party firing"—that is, boss A instructing his assistant B to fire C. This suggests to many of us a lack of nerve, a lack of compassion, or both; it violates the right to cross-examination.

But such a right has not been established as a legal prerogative. And the facts about the weaknesses of interviewing are as Dunnette and Bass have reported. Managers who interview very often—perhaps usually—do it without any special training. Nor do they use the interview in the systematic, probing manner envisioned by our life-history model.

The technical system, then, seems to many psychologists to overcome the subjective and other defects in the other systems. For these reasons, and for the extremely important reason that objective evidence is increasingly supporting the claims of tests, the trend is a strong one. There are, however, these exceptions to it:

■ First, the growth in size in corporations seems to support the bureaucratization of personnel selection methods.

■ Second, because of the equal opportunity trends (not only for minority groups but for women also), there may be an increase in litigation, suits challenging the basis for manager selection as well as selection and promotion decisions made at hourly rated levels.

The incidence of lawsuits would seem to increase the tendency of corporations to use standardized, objective methods for evaluating managerial candidates. While this tendency could reinforce the case for technical selection, it unfortunately also argues for bureaucratic selection; the latter is more likely to prevail because so few industrial managers yet understand the difference between a test or standard that has been proven to work and one that has not. It is generally cheaper to find out whether an applicant has a bona fide college diploma than to find out whether he has measured aptitudes which fit the particular job; the fact that the aptitude measures have been validated for the particular job (at some expense) while the diploma has never been shown to make a difference is not yet impressive to the many managers who are, I am afraid, gullible in matters of personnel selection.

Once again: what is the crucial distinction between bureaucratic standards and technical procedures? Bureaucrats are perfectly willing to use invalidated procedures, while tests have been normally subjected to proof before they are put on the market. It comes as a great surprise to many managers to hear that such hiring standards as number of years of education, IQ scores, and number of years of experience have not been proven valid for most jobs. Folklore tells us many things about qualifications that are not true. For example, research has shown that medical school grades are not related to ability to be a good physician.[11] The power of common sense and folklore is so great, however, that the standards continue to prevail and prevent many good men and women from receiving opportunities.

CAN EXECUTIVE
SELECTION BE IMPROVED?

In the long run, executive selection can be improved by training managers to judge and select people, using the interview to collect systematic life-history data and then making verifiable predictions of human performance. The "batting average" of a manager in making such predictions can be measured in standardized cases (of employees whose performance is known); on this basis, managers who are notably poor at making such predictions should be excluded from influence over the life chances of managerial candidates and other employees.

What, then, is the role of the technical system? Tests can be used to supplement life-history analysis and to serve as a control over a manager's subjectivity. If he deviates too far in his decisions from what the tests suggest they should be, his decisions could be subjected to more detailed scrutiny to determine whether he had let his prejudices sway him too far. Tests should not directly determine a manager's opportunities. In brief, then, it is advocated here that restrictions be put upon the technical system. Just as the x-ray film should not make a decision about surgery, no test should make a decision about job opportunities.

The life-history model of evaluating managers is better suited to the professional and entrepreneurial roles in management. It is the task of such managers to analyze performance anyway. They should become proficient at it. In judging the performance of a manager—which they must do in order to keep control of the company's operation anyway—they are in effect already engaging in a form of life-history assessment. Since it is unavoidable that they will do it, professionals and entrepreneurs should be trained at least as carefully to evaluate human data and make decisions as they are trained to evaluate financial data and make decisions.

chapter nine

Helping Managers Manage

Corporations have long needed a practical diagnostic procedure by which an immediate superior, a consultant, or an associate could sit down with a manager, ask a few sharp questions, determine how things should be done differently, and sharply upgrade that manager's ability. Any person who developed such a diagnostic could practically write his own ticket. He would be a prime candidate for a top managerial post—if top management's function is to help other managers manage.

The conventional name for this diagnostic conference procedure is "performance review." It is not to be confused with supervision, which deals with short-run problems and piecemeal decisions, while performance review is concerned with the longer-run issues and with the job as a whole. The difference is like that between a budget and a particular charge against that budget. Many line managers, when requested the first time to conduct an annual review with a subordinate, confuse this thinking about the job as a whole with thinking about its specific parts. Such a manager may say, "I don't need to do it —after all, I review everyone's work frequently." Such supervision may try to work out ways of improving particular units within a job; but a performance review for that job may show that those problem units need not be done at all.

Performance review poses the most curious problem in organization theory. It is curious because its problems are so contradictory to the hierarchic theory of organization—the theory which assumes that a boss always knows who is performing well and therefore can help him (or direct him) to perform better. If this is true, and this is the curious problem, why is it that the problems of performance review persist? Whisler and Harper [72] reported in 1962 that the prevailing attitude among managers is a paradoxical combination of acute interest and dissatisfaction. Nothing has been reported, since this book, to suggest any substantial improvement, but there are at least two important trends which may lead to solutions:

■ The development of a more realistic form of research. For example, Herbert Meyer [73] at GE actually observed manager-subordinate pairs using different methods of performance appraisal. Twelve to fourteen weeks later, the research team questioned the subordinate to see what the results had been.

■ The continued development and broadening application of "management-by-objectives" (MBO) systems, [74,75] as at SOHIO. MBO appears more consistent with entrepreneurial evaluation than the older performance-review systems.

The central purpose of this chapter is to describe an entrepreneurial approach to performance review and to show how it necessarily contrasts with the older approaches. At the same time, the bureaucratic element in performance review is indispensable. What this means is that using the two approaches, since they are contradictory, will always make performance review difficult.

The Four Models

Performance review, in the autocratic political model, is not logically difficult. This is the system which contends that managers direct others what to do and hold them accountable. As it is an intuitive system, it permits each manager to do it his own way. Under the system there is no reason a fatuous manager may not assume that successes are due to his own correct decisions, and the system permits him to attribute failures to the deficiencies of subordinates. Thus performance review implies detecting error or deviation on the part of the subordinate. The autocrat was intuitive in his appraisal and permitted all kinds of personal notions to creep into the ratings.*

* The following instructions to employees of Marshall Field were issued in 1870: [76]

> "Store will open at 7 a.m. and close at 8 p.m., except on Saturday, when it closes at 9 p.m. Employes [sic] will sweep floors, dust furniture, shelves and show cases; remember 'Cleanliness is next to Godliness.' Trim wicks, fill lamps, clean chimneys. Make your pens carefully (you may whittle the quills to suit your individual taste). Open windows for fresh air. Each clerk shall bring in a bucket of water and a scuttle of coal for the day's business.
>
> "Any employe who smokes Spanish cigars, uses liquor in any form, gets shaved at the barber shop, or frequents pool halls or public dance halls, will give his employer every reason to suspicion his integrity, worthy intentions and all around honesty.
>
> "Each employe is expected to pay his tithing to the church, that is 10% of his annual income; no matter what your income might be, you should not contribute less than $25 per year to the church. Each employe will attend Sacrament meeting and adequate time will be given to attend Fast meeting on Thursday. Also you are expected to attend your Sunday School.
>
> "Men employes will be given one evening off each week for courting purposes, or two evenings each week if they go regularly to church and attend to church duties. After any employe has spent his thirteen hours of labor in the store, he should then spend his leisure time in reading good books, and contemplating the glories and building up the Kingdom of God."

Thus, it was not surprising that early performance-review programs made the mistake of asking supervisors to rate employees on various personal traits (rather than on their performance of various aspects of the work itself).

In the bureaucratic model, some excesses of the autocratic model are dealt with by prescribing the way in which managers will do the performance review. They review performance at certain times, in certain ways, permit subordinates to offer their own views, and may even include a third and objective person in the discussion. At the end of the review, a form may be filled out and signed by all parties. It is unlikely that such a model essentially escapes the basic assumptions of the autocratic models that the purpose of review is to detect errors, and the errors are ordinarily attributed, rightly or wrongly, to the man with lesser power.

The personnel technologists attempted to improve the model quantitatively. Numerous studies have been reported since 1920, showing the statistical effects of using different forms of ratings, of the reliabilities of ratings, and of the possibilities of adding them up to provide an overall estimate of excellence. Curiously, it would not appear, however, that many of the technical and research studies broke free of the bureaucratic assumptions. There are exceptions, as in the work of Flanagan and Burns,[77] showing what kind of performance foremen can actually observe, and Meyer,[73] showing the consequences of different methods of appraisal. In essence, the technological approach to performance review is a quantitative, research-oriented, and predictive approach. It defines the best performance review as that which produces performance increments and other desirable effects.

The entrepreneurial approach to performance review is a goal-setting discussion in which the primary interest is in the future and in those performance results which have effects on the enterprise's results in the environment. The great practical difficulty has been, in the large corporation, relating the work of the individual man to the enterprise's environmental performance.

A SHORT HISTORY
OF PERFORMANCE REVIEW

Why is it so difficult to design performance-review programs which work? Part of the difficulty may lie in the history of performance review itself. Performance review was initially approached as part of the supervisory method appropriate with hourly-paid production and office employees. Features in performance review were developed at that point which were retained, useful or not, for later applications where, I believe, they were emphatically not useful. The general assumption in that era—in the twenties and thirties—was that there is a single best system for doing performance review; it should be transmitted as a matter of policy; people can and should learn to do it through training; the review's findings should be written down. As the prevailing mode of thought about the proper methods of supervision of hourly paid workers was bureaucratic, this came to dominate the design of performance review itself. This was so in the following respects:

1. Performance review was review of work done in the past.

2. It evaluated that work against standards showing how it ought to be done or against other policies.

3. The review was guided by a job description or other paper form.

4. Each part of the job was regarded as a separate entity.

5. Pay was regarded as compensation for what had already been done.

6. Pay was set within a scale which was determined by the relative importance of the job in comparison with others in the organization.

These features of performance review were erroneously retained when personnel departments (which generally designed the review systems in use) were given higher-echelon responsibilities following World War II. Where the personnel department had participated primarily in the selection, training, and other personnel functions in relation to first echelon workers in the twenties and thirties, "management development" came to be a priority following the lessons of the forties. Of what would manager-performance appraisal consist? In its design, personnel men used the bureaucratic features from an earlier time.

A number of innovations during the fifties and sixties were concerned with rejecting these older features. The intuitive vagueness of the old autocratic systems, which had led to the practice of rating moralistic traits (loyalty, cooperation, effort, etc.) instead of performance, was vigorously criticized by Flanagan and Burns;[77] they substituted a system under which employees were observed only in regard to behavioral, specific, concrete performance facts "on which all observers would tend to agree." Results reported for Delco-Remy plants, where their system was used, were excellent; foremen could, and would, use this new system. McGregor's[78] formidable attack on autocratic management led to a number of investigations of what he considered the moral incompatibility of the two tasks involved in performance review: the boss was called upon both to help a person and to judge him. McGregor concluded that "resistance to conventional appraisal programs is eminently sound."

Kellogg[79] described an approach at GE which attempted to solve the problem of vagueness by dealing only with specifics of performance, to minimize the judgmental problem by avoiding discussion of weaknesses, and to reduce the bureaucratic preoccupation with past performance by building performance evaluation around the discussion of goals.

At SOHIO, the resistance of managers to conventional performance appraisal was attributed to these erroneous features: preoccupation with the past, with employee *weaknesses,* and with the idea that a person wants to know how well he is doing. Ohmann [80] had encountered resistance to a system built on these features, and as a result installed a management-by-objectives system there, which managers apparently found far more compatible with their style. The new system made the following assumptions:

■ Managers are in charge of work rather than of people (greatly reducing the autocratic features of the review).

■ Managers cannot change the past, but can meaningfully participate in planning the future.

■ Planning the future means setting goals, and it is goal-setting conferences which ought to be held.

There are many other versions of MBO, but the SOHIO program is as good an example as any.

The current trend in performance review seems to be toward a system of management by objectives. While such a system appears largely consistent with the entrepreneurial model, there are some doubts. These questions should be raised:

■ Is the goal more important to the manager than his personal authority or prestige? (It is not yet clear that MBO has actually rejected the autocratic "do it or else" philosophy of managing.)

■ Is the goal an environmental result, or is it an internal result? (It would seem that MBO could be as well applied to bureaucratic or internally oriented planning of work as well as to external results.)

■ Is MBO merely a technical idea—one designed by personnel departments and industrial engineers—and hence not a true entrepreneurial invention? Or can we find instances in which entire corporations, led vigorously by top managers imbued with the style of MBO (rather than merely "backing it" as a policy), have actively used it to reinvigorate and improve performance?

The answers may be that on all three of these points management by objectives has indeed qualified as an entrepreneurial system, and that the skepticism implied in the questions above is unwarranted. Only research data on the way corporations operate could establish this skepticism as either warranted or unwarranted.

INSTALLING RESULTS-ORIENTED APPRAISAL SYSTEMS

Leaving open for the moment the question of whether management by objectives is truly an entrepreneurial system for evaluating managers, let us consider the more neutral term "results-oriented" performance review. Can we say that managers respond well to this system because it is more natural for them? I think it is not always natural. The following example of corporate resistance to a results-oriented appraisal system might be cited; what managers want to do is not necessarily entrepreneurial or results oriented.

Managerial Resistance

The situation at Western Food Corporation (not its real name) was this. The president wanted to install a performance-review program for his plant and retail-store managers; he believed that he needed to develop managers "on the job" rather than sending them away to executive-development programs. This company planning had been done by a technical planning manager in conjunction with the top management group at the home office in Los Angeles. (This approach is highly disapproved by Drucker, who strongly inveighed against the separation of management and planning.) In fact, one of the company's founders had specifically stated that there was little difficulty in being a company manager unless a manager was located in the home office; pricing, manufacturing, and distribution policies were the difficult planning decisions, and managers in outlying plants and retail stores merely had to carry out these decisions. If the latter did their jobs properly, the company would turn out good products, maintain good customer relations, and make a profit.

There was little to be done about this official's attitude of contempt for his managers. But the company's vice-president of organization recognized that the nub of the performance-review problem was the need of greater respect for managers and their involvement in at least some aspects of the planning operation. The company's subsequent reasoning was that a bureaucratic review of each manager's successes and failures during the previous year was far less to the point than the setting of better objectives for which he and his immediate superior would be accountable in the following year.

The chief resistance to involving managers in planning came eventually from the managers themselves. Most of the plant and retail-store managers viewed the new system with considerable unease. They didn't like the old review system either (they were simply given a rating by their boss as to how well they were planning, coordinating, delegating, and controlling). But the new one was greeted with evasion, minimal compliance, and dilatoriness.

The elements in the new plan which apparently aroused the most apprehension were:

1. The company asked each manager to state, in advance, how much cost control he could exert in each major area of his operation for the coming year.

2. It asked him to state how much of his resources would go into market expansion (looking for new customers) as opposed to market consolidation (taking care of the old ones), and what sales results he expected for the coming year.

3. It asked him to forecast sales potentiality for *five* years in advance, within a geographic area which it specified for him.

4. It asked him to indicate the production capacity which would be required for that sales potentiality.

5. If he was a plant manager, it asked him to indicate the costs of achieving that production capacity.

The greatest resistance was to being "nailed down," being held accountable for new things. Curiously enough, these managers had long felt accountable for profits and sales volume. They expected to be "punished" when both were down, even if the entire market was down (i.e., even if they had no real control over the profit and sales volume). They preferred the more irrational system under which they were already working, but which they understood, to a more rational system which was relatively unclear to them. Western's new system did not lessen managers' responsibility for sales and profits, but it did make the responsibility more *contingent*—for example, if a manager failed to reduce his production costs because the *company* did not provide new equipment, the new system made him less accountable than the old. But he was *more* accountable for those kinds of costs which *he* could control—even when profits were good.

A second difficulty lay in the area of prediction. The managers felt—with some justification—that they were being asked to make forecasts. They were assured of staff help in making forecasts and further assured that the type of plan involved was a "rolling plan" which would be revised whenever new data clearly required it (annually at minimum). Nevertheless, a typical complaint was, "I don't have a crystal ball." Another said, "Our interest is profits not prophets."

A third difficulty resulted from prior work habits. These managers had come up through the ranks, doing jobs in which they were accountable for day-to-day matters and in which the supervision they received was bureaucratic in nature. They had learned to absorb themselves in their work;

many earnestly put in long hours but in a somewhat mindless way. (For example, on tasks which produced little return for the company because the company had designated those tasks as primary.) Over the years, this particular company had had a favorable market position, community image, and little competition. It had made a great deal of money. The managers, bureaucratic or not, were being paid quite well. They drove big cars and joined exotic California clubs. They felt they had earned their money because they had worked long, hard hours. When anyone questioned the "system," their answer was, "It has always made money, hasn't it?"

These managers were not especially open to the critical suggestions of outside consultants, or even of their own home office. The old system had paid them to believe in itself. When the times changed, bringing tighter conditions, their response was to work harder and to drive their people harder.

After some backing and filling, Western Corporation made the new planning system stick. Most of the older managers continued to maintain that they had done well enough on the old system, while the younger ones showed enthusiasm for the new ways.

An interpretation. The Western Food Corporation example is more than an illustration of resistance to change. Resistance to the planning function is itself a problem. Historically, Americans have always resisted planning—not only by others for themselves but by themselves also. An executive once told me he thought managerial planning was "socialistic." This resistance can be explained in part by some American experiences with planning. But in part, it has to do also with the psychological aspects of planning itself. To do planning, one has to undergo a period of initial ambiguity in which he is faced with a complex, rather formless and confusing future. One may escape this future shock by doing a competent job of planning (thus replacing the confusion with an orderly "map" of the future) or by running away from it. One may run away from the future and end the uncertainty by burying himself in his work, in the day-to-day routines of his job—this is what most of the Western Food managers did. The point, then, is that planning is not only a technically difficult managerial task (books are written about it) but also an *emotional* problem (no one writes books about this part of it). As a rough guess, I would say that the emotional part of it causes the greater resistance than the technical difficulties of planning.

Such managerial resistance to the planning function (implied in management by objectives and in the entrepreneurial model of management) is handled just like any other resistance to change (see Chapter 2).

Entrepreneurial Evaluation

Every large institution goes through periodic misery, even travail, in searching for a more equitable performance-review system. During World War II many generals who had reached their posts of eminence through the peacetime "officer-fitness" evaluations had to be removed during battle.* It is sometimes maintained that, unlike government and the peacetime military, business has "an easy time of it" because, after all, it possesses economic yardsticks. If a manager does not show a profit, out he goes! Such statements represent the Sunday-Supplement level of analysis; they are a travesty and a dangerous fiction.

In the first place, there is a large and growing list of specialties which cannot, by any remote stretch of the imagination, be judged against profit. In the second place, even a general manager cannot be judged accurately by the imperfect financial yardsticks which are available. It is true that stockholders

---

* This was stated to me informally by a high-ranking military officer whose primary function following the Normandy landing was to shuttle back and forth from headquarters to the front, where his task was to oversee the removal of ranking officers judged incompetent. It was an unpleasant task, and I doubt that he would care to be identified.

and others may go hunting for the head of a president whose operation (like United Air Lines in 1970) is losing large sums of money. The *politics* of business are financial; and the politics cannot be ignored. But this is not to say that these politics are rational.

For those who wish to do the hard thinking required to understand business, Peter Drucker has made use of economic measurements rather clear. Financial yardsticks are needed for part of enterprise evaluation but are not the whole of it. Some conglomerate corporations exist in which the home office is *said* to maintain *only* financial controls over the different divisions—this is unsound to the extent that managers are evaluated on a purely financial basis.

Work in an enterprise system is judged in an extraordinarily complex, subtle, and, at some points, inescapably intuitive manner. It is unlikely that a quantitative formula stating conditions under which this or that president should be removed or promoted will ever be written. This point should be obvious to anyone who has ever participated in the selection of a president.* However, the complex, subtle, and intuitive nature of this judgment does not mean it is lacking in discipline. To evaluate a person in a complex managerial job, one practically has to write a business case, covering the qualitative (and some quantitative) events of his regime. This point is more than analogy and is here intended literally. The *intellectual* disciplines underlying the collection and interpretation of managerial-performance data are very similar to the preparation and interpretation of a business case history.

Logic and method of case preparation. For all the cases that have been written, very little has been written about the methods of investigation, data gathering, and presentation of findings used. Some cases published appear to be serious presenta-

---

* See "Debate at Wickersham Mills"; [81] the research report of Glickman, et al., is particularly informative. [67]

tions of fact, and some appear to be intriguing teaching devices not held to be authentic or carefully documented. What is meant here is the collection of narrative accounts of what has happened (in a department, division, or corporation), including—but certainly not limited to—quantified data, as objective as possible but not excluding impressionistic data. For the purposes of appraising managers, a case must tell not only what happened over the time period, but who did what, and how each significant decision eventuated in results of relevance to corporate goals.

The documentation of manager appraisal. Each manager should prepare an annual (or other appropriate time period) report similar in form to the corporate report to the stockholders. However, it would be more technical and include more detail on what decisions were made and what the consequences were. This document is the basis for his appraisal. He should be cross-examined regarding its completeness and accuracy and implications. This procedure seems as fair in appraising managers as it is fair to evaluate the corporation president on the basis of the corporate annual report. It is equally relevant.

The function of ratings. No "numbers games" should be played in such appraisal. This need not deny the desirability of ratings for research purposes. But the applicability of quantification for describing complex performance has been greatly overstated. One can see no more reason for rating a manager than for rating concert pianists, presidential contenders, or playwrights. For example, the music critic writes a column of critical appraisal after a concert; he does not award a "3" to the pianist or debate whether perhaps he really ought to merit a "2." It is true that we cannot escape quantification in two respects: how much we will pay the manager and whether he will be retained or not (the latter being a Yes/No decision). These are quantities, and perhaps it might be argued that they are actually ratings.

The entrepreneurial approach to performance review for managers sets future goals for the individual manager in the context of the overall enterprise's future course. Management by objective is a long stride toward such an entrepreneurial approach, but it is not yet certain that it is identical with it. To develop an entrepreneurial evaluation approach for a particular company, one must cope with the emotional as well as intellectual difficulties managers have with planning.

The entrepreneurial approach involves disciplines similar to the preparation of a document very similar to a first-rate business case. The end product of this preparation is a document which resembles an annual report in content (with less PR and more fact).

How is such a document used to help a manager manage? First, it should be cross-examined—no matter who wrote it! Second, it should result in a plan for the following time period, a set of goals which are frankly discussed and mutually agreed upon. Third, it is kept as a running record of the manager's experience. The logic of evaluating the entrepreneurial manager is the same as the logic of the president's annual report to the stockholders. If *he* has to do it, all his managers should do it; he is the first among entrepreneurs, not the one and only entrepreneur.

chapter ten

The New Entrepreneur

In this book I have tried to describe the human situation of the manager who wishes to work at the heart of the kind of enterprise we are seeing develop in the last third of the twentieth century. It is easy enough to see that this manager is not a bureaucrat; the bureaucrat is on the fringe rather than at the heart of his firm. This new entrepreneur can be described most easily by contrast with the manager of the last century. That image was, according to a number of historians, opportunistic, money grubbing, aggressive, and autocratic. Whether that image was ever valid or not, some of these traits do seem to have echoes in the new entrepreneur. We should note that some entrepreneurs in this new mold already exist; the future will be characterized by more such managers.

In spite of occasional research papers hopefully reporting that the new manager is not so interested in making money, we assume this interest has not gone out of style. That part of the old image remains. But the role played by money in his motivations is somewhat different. It does not require a huge amount of money to move a person out of the low- or middle-income group, up to the point at which he can afford the luxury of an affluent outlook, and "eu-stress" is largely a luxury for the affluent. Of course, the entrepreneur must be able to think that large returns *might* well come his way, and occasionally someone must hit a jackpot to keep the game credible. In brief, then, the entrepreneur is a well-paid person who can dream credibly about making much more money "if things work out."

The "money" image changes when we ask how the entrepreneur is to be judged. Whether or not we could determine a nineteenth-century manager's effectiveness by his money-making ability, it is most certainly true now that corporation presidents cannot be judged by this factor alone. Their purpose is to increase the assets or resources of a corporation for the long pull. Profit is the central measure of this increase, but to use it in isolation from others is to misunderstand the peculiar genius of the corporation. Thus the role of money is still important but somewhat more subtle than was true in the last century.

A second feature in the old managerial image was aggressiveness. He was tough, remorseless, tenacious, insistent on his way. The new entrepreneur also needs these qualities; management is still a power game. But the way in which these traits are used and blended must be different. The autocrat (see p. 190) is dead. There can be no more Henry Fords.

This change has been perhaps obscured by the fact that

management continues to demand very great quantities of a person's energy. Energetic people *appear* aggressive to others. But the energy of eu-stress, as I have noted, is not the energy of a person who pushes others around simply for the sake of gratifying his power urges. David Ewing pointed this out when he suggested "tension can be an asset."[82] He doubted that harmonious organizations and satisfied workers should be high on any manager's priority list. He used an image of Duncan Littlefair's to describe the eu-stress of organizational life: ". . . a sailboat makes headway because of the opposition of its sail to the wind. If this opposition is firm, the sailboat makes good speed . . . [if] too strong, . . . the boat may keel over."

In brief, then, the very considerable energetic quality that I[58] have noted in the accounts of eminent business executives is essential to the new entrepreneurial manager, and it is attributed here to the freedom enjoyed by the manager who is oriented to eu-stress rather than to dys-stress. Stress is the spice of this manager's life. He turns on in his work, not only because of the money he finds (or thinks he may find) in it but also because of the "opposition of the sail to the wind." Young college students who speak of turning on are closer to this new entrepreneur than are their overworked, overburdened, and dys-stressed fathers.

THE NEW ENTREPRENEUR'S THINKING

The new manager must be more intellectual than the old entrepreneur. Not smarter, but more intellectual. The information channels he needs to maintain contact with trends in the environment are far more numerous, abstract, and intellectually demanding than his great-grandfather's data. The new entrepreneur has more in common with college professors than he does with the small-town Rotary Club member.

Where the nineteenth-century capitalist was a schemer, a man looking for an angle (in brief, opportunistic), the new entrepreneur is a planner, a scenario writer, a futurist. The impulse is much the same, but the thinking is more elaborate. Accounts now available in family traditions and journalistic writings of the nineteenth century portray the old-timers as thoughtless, though somehow canny, gamblers. No one can afford this rather careless approach today; the environment is too complex for it to work.

The new manager must think in terms of "open systems." This intricate method of thought, which embraces the internal corporate structure and the external environmental dynamics under one system of concepts, is so new that little has yet been written about it, and less of that is clearly stated. The output of this thought is a "scenario" rather than a scheme. A scenario is a complex plan of action which states its assumptions about the environment, is conscious of the structural relationships among goals in real-time, and is flexible rather than rigid. It is futuristic, often deeply so. The *schemer* was usually a short-term man, sometimes even a confidence man. The scenario writer *can* write short-term plans of action, but he is more likely to find opportunities in the longer-range perspective which others fear or cannot master.

The old entrepreneur was an intuitive operator with little self-awareness. The new entrepreneur writes scenarios for his own career as well as for his organization. Most of the eminent men whose careers I have studied seemed to know their individual goals as well as those of their corporations. Granted, these eminent men were born in or near the turn of the century. They were self-aware rather than self-preoccupied. There is an important difference. The self-aware man has a picture of his career, based on occasional reflection. The preoccupied man has a set of problems which dys-stress him. The eu-stressed man is open to his future (Maslow [50]), and the dys-stressed man keeps going over his past. The one man reads Maslow, the other man Freud.

In brief, the new entrepreneurial "maps of the future" have these characteristics:

- both internal (answering such questions as "How will the plan use and expand the assets of this corporation?") and external ("How will it take advantage of trends and opportunities in the environment?") characteristics
- both business and personal orientations
- a longer timeline (reaching further into the future) than the old-fashioned business scheme or "sales campaign"

THE INNOVATIONS LIKELY TO RESULT

There is a tendency to classify entrepreneurs as innovators. There is much truth in this classification, but the new entrepreneur is still a special breed. He is not just a schemer or inventor who works for the corporation; he is more a manager who is inventive. His innovations must be economically feasible—they are not just new patents—and they must affect the organization's environment (entrepreneurial innovations are *not* new ways to save paper clips in the office). They must do something human in the environment (e.g., not just build large planes to be building large planes). Human needs and services are more the measure of these new innovations than are technical feasibility and challenge.

This concern is the primary distinction between the entrepreneur and the R&D man. The entrepreneur has an edge over the R&D man in knowing something about the human system which makes up society. He is probably interested in the new possibilities of technology, but not until they promise some kind of human benefit or relevance. It is quite possible that, in most societies, entrepreneurs will be tolerated politically only if they adopt this point of view. I am not stating whether or not this condition is desirable but rather predicting that it will soon be fact if it is not so already.

In brief, the entrepreneur will see that many things are technically possible and economically promising but still not humanly worth doing. If he does not learn to see this, political interests will probably begin to make this decision for him. If the reign of the pure capitalist was over by 1930 (Burnham [47]), the reign of the technologically opportunistic enterprise is swiftly drawing to an end in the 1970s.

THE NEW ENTREPRENEURIAL STYLE

The old entrepreneur was said to be an individualist, an autocrat, and a directive s.o.b. who pushed people around. He occasionally went to autocratic excess. This kind of loner usually cannot thrive in the big corporation world. Indeed, some corporations are so big and so international that the new manager may well have to develop and master the arts of corporate statecraft. Autocratic management is out, not because participative management works better but simply because the new entrepreneur is, by definition, nonautocratic. The *style* has changed. The new entrepreneur is a man who judges performance not according to obedience but according to results. The logic of this incompatibility is not difficult to follow. The autocrat *knew* that his plans were correct; if they failed, it was because *employees* did not do what they were supposed to do. The entrepreneur, by contrast, does not know whether his plans are correct (he knows that the future is ambiguous and uncertain) until there is a result.

The new entrepreneur must clearly face and solve new problems of authority in the corporation. For many reasons, including the rise in the average employee's educational level, directive authority cannot be used as before. The search for new bases of authority is on; early impressions suggest that the new authority comes from goals. Thus motivation is through the "pulling power" of the future rather than the "pushing power" of a boss or the moralistic requirements of a bureaucrat. The new entrepreneur tries to use the eu-stress style with others as well as with himself. It may, of course, be too much to expect that the less-than-affluent person will enjoy the eu-stresses of business. We may hope for this result one day, but we may certainly not expect or demand it. In a company which cannot pay well, autocracy and bureaucracy cannot be completely eliminated.

Indeed, bureaucracy should not be eliminated. Orderly rules and regulations provide a comfortable security and can even be efficient. One wants bureaucratic efficiency to handle his airline tickets; no one wants less than an ironclad bureaucratic control of cleanliness, etc., in the room where he is undergoing surgery. All managers should not be entrepreneurs; just the key ones.

More people will follow the new entrepreneur because this kind of manager can radiate more charisma than can the bureaucrat, autocrat, or technologist. I do not claim he will be better liked or loved, only that he can lead by setting forth imaginative goals. In this sense, the new breed of entrepreneur foreshadows a return to "romanticism." We are already seeing a new romanticism in colleges, and I think we will find it shortly in the board rooms. As hair lengthened, first among college students and then among executives, as shirts became more garishly colored among students and then executives, so we are also seeing transmission of new life styles from young to old. This change may be appalling or appealing; but whichever it is has nothing to do with whether the prediction is accurate.

The romantic conception of business visualizes leaders who are heroes to their people. This follows the eu-stress line of reasoning: the manager who does things which turn him on, which open up opportunities for his firm, and whose management style is highly visible to others who are "identified" with the firm will be a hero of sorts.

THE MORAL STATURE
OF THE NEW ENTREPRENEUR

The term "heroic" is used advisedly because we usually insist that the hero be a fighter for good ends. Nowhere in this book have I suggested that entrepreneurs are good or that they are bad. They are too individualistic for "quickie" judgment. (Others will, however, eventually make such judgments anyway.)

Eventually the entrepreneur, as a type, will be considered by most people as very, very good or very, very bad. Risk takers must operate in a very visible way. Their errors and their successes will be quite public. By contrast, the bureaucrat is a creature of policy; he makes no decisions, takes no stands, incurs no risks. Hence it may become true that bureaucrats, because professional in manner and dedicated in outlook, will generally be esteemed by the public. It is too early to predict whether entrepreneurs will be villains or heroes. It is likely that they will be classified, individually, according to the effects of their policies. If, as a class, they are defined as villainous, they may well be legislated out of existence. We will then be ruled by bureaucrats, which is to say, by policies which no one wrote and for which no one can be blamed. These gentle, kindly, and well-intentioned men will not bring us Orwell's fascist future—

> If you want a picture of the future, imagine a boot stamping on a human face—forever.

But they will bring us the life which Weber once described:

It is horrible to think that the world could one day be filled with nothing but those little cogs, little men clinging to little jobs and striving toward bigger ones . . . to become men who need 'order' and nothing but order, who become nervous and cowardly if for one moment this order wavers, and helpless if they are torn away from their total incorporation in it.[83]

Note: Related Readings

1. Servan-Schreiber, J. H., *The American Challenge*, New York: Avon, 1969.
2. Koontz, H., "The Management Theory Jungle," *Journal of the Academy of Management*, vol. 4, no. 3, December 1961, pp. 174–188.
3. Drucker, P. F., *Managing for Results*, New York: Harper & Row, 1964.
4. Dale, E., *The Great Organizers*, New York: McGraw-Hill, 1960.
5. Smith, R. A., *Corporations in Crisis*, Garden City, N.Y.: Doubleday, 1963.
6. Blau, P. M., *The Dynamics of Bureaucracy*, Chicago: University of Chicago Press, 1955.
7. Blau, P. M., and W. R. Scott, *Formal Organizations: A Comparative Approach*, San Francisco: Chandler, 1962.
8. Dailey, C. A., G. H. Carlson, and M. R. McChesney, *The Projects CAUSE: An Evaluation*, Washington (Department of Labor), 1968.
9. Subcommittee on Manpower and Civil Service (Committee on Post Office and Civil Service, House of Representatives), Report no. 329, 1967.

10. Craig, R. L., and L. R. Bittel (eds.), *Training and Development Handbook*, New York: McGraw-Hill, 1967.

11. Taylor, C. W., P. B. Price, J. M. Richards, Jr., R. T. Jacobsen, "An Investigation of the Criterion Problem for a Group of Medical General Practitioners," *Journal of Applied Psychology*, vol. 49, no. 6, December 1965, pp. 399–406.

12. Lanvin, David E., *Predicting Academic Performance*, New York: Russell Sage, 1965.

13. Drucker, P. F., *The Practice of Management*, New York: Harper & Row, 1954.

14. Dale, E., "André Malraux and the Problem of Change," *MSU Business Topics*, Spring, 1967, pp. 7–10.

15. Whyte, W. H., Jr., *The Organization Man*, New York: Simon and Schuster, 1956.

16. Malraux, André, *Man's Hope*, New York: Random House, 1938 (Scali), p. 391.

17. Toffler, Alvin, *Future Shock*, New York: Random House, 1970.

18. Barber, R. J., *The American Corporation*, New York: Dutton, 1970, p. 27.

19. Klausner, S., *Why Man Takes Chances*, Garden City, N.Y.: Doubleday, 1968.

20. Drucker, P. F., *The Effective Executive*, New York: Harper & Row, 1966.

21. Millis, W., *Arms and the Man*, New York: Putnam, 1950.

22. Berelson, B., and G. Steiner, *Human Behavior*, New York: Harcourt, Brace & World, 1964.

23. Greenberg, D. S., "The Odd Couple, Strains in Science, Engineering Academies," *Science*, Oct. 30, 1970, vol. 170, no. 3957, p. 513.

24. Alinsky, S., *New York Times*, Fall 1970.

25. Szasz, T., *The Myth of Mental Illness*, New York: Hoeber-Harper, 1964.

26. Albee, G., 1970 Presidential Address, American Psychological Association Convention, Miami Beach, Fla.

27. Silver, Isidore, "The Corporate Ombudsman," *Harvard Business Review*, May–June 1967, p. 77.

28. Walton, R., *Interpersonal Peacemaking: Confrontation and Third Party Consultation*, Reading, Mass.: Addison-Wesley, 1969.

29. Nicolson, Sir H., *Diplomacy*, New York: Oxford, 1964.

30. Jay, A., *Money and Machiavelli*, New York: Holt, 1968.

31. Simon, H., *Administrative Behavior*, New York: Macmillan, 1947.

32. Likert, R., *New Patterns of Management*, New York: McGraw-Hill, 1961.

33. McGregor, D., *The Human Side of Enterprise*, New York: McGraw-Hill, 1960.

34. Schelling, T. C., *The Strategy of Conflict*, New York: Oxford, 1963.

35. Boulding, K., *Organizational Revolution,* New York: Harper, 1953.
36. Selye, H., *The Stress of Life,* New York: McGraw-Hill, 1956.
37. Holmes, T., and R. H. Rahe, "The Social Readjustment Rating Scale," *Journal of Psychosomatic Research,* vol. 11, 1967, p. 213.
38. Rubin, S. A., "The Personal Price of National Glory," *Trans-Action,* vol. 2, no. 6, September–October 1965, p. 4.
39. Levinson, H., *Executive Stress,* New York: Harper & Row, 1964 (rev. 1970).
40. Hausmann, J. P., *Stress,* Bern, Switzerland: Paul Haupt, 1970 (in German).
41. Bernard, J., "The Eudaemonists," in *Why Man Takes Chances* by S. Klausner. Garden City, N.Y.: Doubleday, 1968.
42. Herzberg, F., *The Motivation to Work,* New York: Wiley, 1967.
43. Brinton, C., *Nietzsche,* Cambridge: Harvard, 1941, p. 134.
44. Miner, J. B., *Studies in Management Education,* New York: Springer, 1965.
45. Veblen, T. B., *Theory of the Leisure Class,* New York: Macmillan, 1899.
46. Fromm, E., *Man For Himself,* New York: Rinehart, 1947.
47. Burnham, J., *The Managerial Revolution: What Is Happening in the World?* New York: John Day, 1941.
48. Leavitt, H. J., and T. L. Whisler, "Management in the 1980's," *Harvard Business Review,* vol. 36, no. 6, 1958, pp. 13–27.
49. "The Causes of Student Protest," *The President's Commission on Student Unrest* (The Scranton Report), 1970.
50. Maslow, A., "Peak Experience in Education and Art, *The Humanist,* September–October 1970, pp. 29–31.
51. Kazantzakis, Nikos, *Zorba the Greek,* New York: Simon and Schuster, 1953.
52. Bower, M., *The Will to Manage,* New York: McGraw-Hill, 1966.
53. Patton, A., *Men, Money and Motivation,* New York: McGraw-Hill, 1961.
54. Homans, G. C., *Sentiments and Activities,* New York: Free Press, 1962.
55. Roman, D. D., "The PERT System: An Appraisal of Program Evaluation Review Technique," *Journal of Academy of Management,* April 1962, pp. 57–65.
56. Michael, D. N., *The Unprepared Society: Planning for a Precarious Future,* New York: Harper & Row, 1968.
57. Gardner, J. W., "How to Prevent Organizational Dry Rot," Copyright © 1965, by Minneapolis Star and Tribune Co., Inc. Reprinted from the October, 1965, issue of *Harper's Magazine* by permission of the author.
58. Dailey, C. A., "The Longitudinal Analysis of the Personalities of Eminent Leaders," *Proceedings of the Fifteenth International Congress of*

Psychology, Brussels (1957), Amsterdam: North-Holland Publishing Co., 1959, pp. 446–447.

59. Hansen, G. A., "Britain's Industrial Training Act: Is It Working?" *Training and Development Journal*, August 1969.

60. Lippert, F., "British Management Training Today and Tomorrow," *Training and Development Journal*, April 1970.

61. Frank, H. E., "Management Development in Eastern Europe," *Training and Development Journal*, April 1970.

62. Bois, J. S., "Levels of Cultural Communication," *ETC.*, vol. 13, no. 4, 1955–56, p. 272.

63. Emery, D. H., *The Compleat Manager*, New York: McGraw-Hill, 1970.

64. Strauss, L. L., *Men and Decisions*, New York: Popular, 1963 (Doubleday, 1962).

65. Peter, L. J., and R. Hull, *The Peter Principle*, New York: Morrow, 1969.

66. Caplow, T., and R. J. McGee, *The Academic Marketplace*, New York: Science Editions, Basic Books, 1961.

67. Glickman, A. S., C. P. Hahn, E. H. Fleishman, B. Baxter, *Top Management Development and Succession*, New York: Committee for Economic Development, 1968.

68. Meyer, J. A., *Predicting Managerial Success*, Ann Arbor, Mich.: Foundation for Research on Human Behavior, 1968.

69. Dailey, C. A., *The Assessment of Lives*, San Francisco: Jossey-Bass, 1971 (in press).

70. Cronbach, L. J., and G. C. Gleser, *Psychological Tests and Personnel Decisions*, Urbana: University of Illinois Press, 1965.

71. Dunnette, M. D., and B. M. Bass, "Behavioral Scientists and Personnel Management," *Industrial Relations*, vol. 2, no. 3, May, 1963. Reprinted in Wortman, Max, *Creative Personnel Management*, Boston: Allyn and Bacon, 1967, pp. 336–350.

72. Whisler, T., and S. F. Harper, *Performance Appraisal*, New York: Holt, 1962.

73. Meyer, H. H., E. Kay, and J. R. P. French, "Split Roles in Performance Appraisal," *Harvard Business Review*, vol. 43, no. 1, 1965, pp. 123–129.

74. Ivancevich, J. M., "The Theory and Practice of M-b-O," *Michigan Business Review*, March 1969.

75. Odiorne, G. S., "Management by Objectives—The Current State of the Art," paper given at American Psychological Association, Sept., 1970.

76. Attributed to an early store manual of Marshall Field by O. A. Ohmann in a speech before the Industrial Relations Association of Cleveland, 1946.

77. Flanagan, J. C., and R. K. Burns, "The Employee Performance Record," *Harvard Business Review*, Spetember–October 1957, pp. 95–102.

78. McGregor, D., "An Uneasy Look at Performance Appraisal," *Harvard Business Review*, May–June 1957, pp. 89–94.
79. Kellogg, M. S., "New Angles in Appraisal," in Whisler, T., and S. F. Harper, *Performance Appraisal*, New York: Holt, pp. 88–95.
80. Ohmann, O. A., "Management Development in a Functional Type of Organization," paper presented to the National Industrial Conference Board, New York, Jan. 21, 1960.
81. Collier, A. T., "Debate at Wickersham Mills," *Harvard Business Review*, May–June 1960, p. 49.
82. Ewing, D., "Tension Can Be an Asset," *Harvard Business Review*, October 1964, p. 71.
83. Bendix, R., *Max Weber: An Intellectual Portrait*, Garden City, N.Y.: Doubleday, 1960, pp. 455–456.

Index

Index